# Growing Up
# PARANORMAL

# Growing Up
# PARANORMAL

Donna Parish-Bischoff

Cover Design: Donna Davies
Interior Design: Donna Davies
Publisher: DPB Publishing
ISBN-13: 978-0615857152
ISBN-10: 0615857159
Printed in United States

Cover Models:
Emma Halstead
Rose Halstead
Ava Paradiso

# CONTENTS

# SPIRITS AMONG US

# DEDICATION

I would like to dedicate this book to anyone who has been on this journey alongside me, whether you know me personally, or not.

If you are reading this, it says that you are a part of this unique club for which we have membership. Sometimes we travel a hard, learned road, a long time before we realize there is a room full of individuals just like ourselves. In that, we find comfort and friendship.

I find it is better to make yourself known, and introduce yourself, as who you are, for there is that small percentage of people, who have been waiting to meet you, to exchange their stories. We teach and learn each day, and for that, I am grateful for every one of you.

# ACKNOWLEDGEMENTS

It is with great love, respect, and friendship that I bring the following names and their stories to life on the pages on this book. For well over a year, I reached out in good faith asking them to join me in this journey.

With a leap of faith they trusted in me and chose to share their stories. I cherish them for this, and appreciate each and every one of them. I know how important it is to have these experiences and how hard it is to come out and share some of these special moments with another living being...let alone the rest of the world. It means more than any word that has ever been invented to date to speak from my lips what this means to me, asking those to join me in this journey.

These souls have honored their loved ones by sharing their lives journeys and experiences with me and with you. I have enjoyed reading them and I am sure the rest of the world will share my sentiments and feelings as well. We all have this common thread we share in life.

So without further ado I would like to list all the wonderful spirits that made this book come alive to share their life experiences with all of us. And again, thanks to all of you for being a part of something bigger than we understand.

# FORWARD

Donna Parish-Bischoff offers a vividly, visually pleasing experience as she recounts her life, encountering spirits throughout, as her loved ones passed. She touches upon dreams, and on how she believes in messages from beyond the grave.

The author is personal in her own experiences, which leads the reader to the thoughts of what happens in death to our body. There is a curiosity to this subject matter and in today's upsurge of hobbyists doing paranormal investigations, a much-welcomed tone.

Several people have submitted to the book in-order to give a full comprehension of other's experiences and outcomes. The author gives a poignant emphasis on a faith-believed opinion that we do indeed, go somewhere, after we die.

Spiritually uplifting and well written, this is a good read for anyone searching to understand that we are not alone in life and in death. We do go on and we do continue our Spirit.

-- Author and Ghost Hunter, Alexandra Holzer

# PREFACE

This book takes you through not only my own life's unique experiences but a journey of many.

Collectively we decided to share with you, the readers some of the most intimate moments we encountered with the unknown. Some call us brave, some call us crazy. We like to think of ourselves as blessed and lucky.

For beyond the dimensions of so many layers of existence, there is something far greater, beyond our comprehension. As a child I was frightened because I just didn't know, didn't understand. I grew into a woman that grabbed on and refused to let go of what this great force of energy was and continues to be the Holy Grail we long to discover.

This book takes you by the hand as it shares the tender, emotional, journey of what most of us experience. There are a large percentage of people that have these awakenings yet they will dismiss it and never share it. They will discard of the experience thinking they will be ridiculed for talking about their experience.

Hopefully this book will help others know they are not alone. We all belong to this club. There is no membership fee.

I welcome you with open arms to join us and embrace what you thought was your imagination. There are no coincidences after all.

# CHAPTER ❧1❧

## IN THE BEGINNING

I normally find that after I write or speak about the paranormal I get the best of both the flip sides. I get the ones who embrace it with love and respect, and are eager to share their stories with me as well as hear my stories of the paranormal. Then there are the ones who assume I am money hungry and whistle bullshit out of my ass. If you take five minutes to get to know me, you will know which one I am.

I welcome both types of people. It allows me to introduce myself and it lets people get to know me. I accept them as they wish to be accepted and they can accept me as I am. Nothing more, I play with pretty simple rules.

I want each of these chapters to be as if I were to have invited you into my home, and made you a cup of coffee. Let's pretend I started to personally take you on this journey through my life, and shared some of the experiences of those of my friend's as well.

Let's begin that journey shall we? I am about to share some of my very personal stories. Some that really gave me a clear sense that there is an existence, after we pass on. This brought me much comfort. I believe we are given signs that keep us a float until our time is ready. We are given these comforting signs from a song on the radio, to a smile from a stranger, or a butterfly that appears to be following you. Only you know for sure it's more than a song, a smile, and a butterfly. It's a sign. Your life may be spiraling downward, but there will be a lyric to a song, that you never heard before, that captures your attention, at that right moment. It's a higher power working to let you know you are not alone. You were meant to hear that at that moment.

Everything has a perfect timing for a reason my friend. Your loved ones may have gone on before you, but they are not far from you. They are at wings length. Do not worry I do not preach in this book. But I have had close calls. I have seen many things, and heard many things, not to know, and understand these things.

And I would be a, (in plain English, a dumb ass) not to let you all in on this special message if you already don't know it.

Keep the faith, whatever faith you follow.

So pour that cup of coffee, settle in with this book, and enjoy the experience.

# CHAPTER ෨2෨

## GROWING UP PARANORMAL

In the years that followed, it became more evident to me that there was an afterlife. Sometimes not so *happily ever after* either. I became obsessed with death and the significance of its role. Some believe that it's lights out—no more. We have no souls. No Heaven. No Hell. I feel as if no one really has the real answer. The only thing I can firmly sit here and tell you is there is something out there.

As you know, or probably already know, energy never dies. It changes into endless forms. It has the gift of infinity. (The gift that keeps on giving.) Some spirits, for reasons that are unknown, linger after they die. Maybe they have some unfinished business, or are scared to go into the light; given there is one. Maybe they can't leave a loved one.

I wish I could sit here and give you all the answers you wanted regarding the afterlife, but like you, I am still learning. With every roaming spirit it's a new experience. Ghosts are like snowflakes to me. Every one of them is unique and different. In any case you are faced with, you have to perform your investigation with the utmost respect.

I laugh to myself when I watch some of these paranormal shows and see other investigative teams claim to have the "Holy Grail" of answers concerning the spirit world and paranormal research. I have always said and felt the need to learn as much as we can from one another when it comes to paranormal investigating. Some equipment may work wonders for one investigation and have zilch effect on another. It's all trial and error. So, you see it's not all a black and white, open and shut case. Sometimes there is no label for a particular situation. Together we go on a journey, share each other's experiences, knowledge, and wisdom of what we have learned. It's all an educational experience and each one is a wonderful and exciting expedition

It's heartbreaking to lose a loved one. We feel a sense of loss. Our bodies go through hell during our physical existence. Our health deteriorates, we suffer from depression, our appetites wane, and our internal organs take the brunt of our emotional mourning. The human body can actually die from this process. You may have heard; "a person died of a broken heart" or a person "pined away for the deceased loved one". This is yet another quest for my obsession with the afterlife— investigating. To explore the energy that resonates after one passes away.

On April 10, 1901, an unusual experiment was conducted in Dorchester, Massachusetts. Dr. Duncan MacDougall was going to prove that the human soul had mass, and was therefore, measurable. Dr. MacDougall conducted this experiment on six dying patients who were placed on specially made Fairbanks weight scales just prior to their deaths. Dr. MacDougall's intention was to weigh each body before and after death to determine any differences measured by the delicate scales. The patients were selected based upon their imminent death.. Two patients were suffering from tuberculosis; 5 were men, and one was a woman.

In the company of four other doctors, Dr. MacDougall carefully measured the weight of his first patient prior to his death. Once the patient died, an interesting event occurred. *"Suddenly, coincident with death,"* wrote MacDougall, *"the beam end dropped with an audible stroke hitting against the lower limiting bar and remaining there with no rebound. The loss was ascertained to be three-fourths of an ounce."* [1] The experiment continued on the next patient with the same results. Dr. MacDougall felt he was on to something extraordinary. A quote from the 11 March 1907 New York Times article captures the historic moment:

*"The instant life ceased the opposite scale pan fell with a suddenness that was astonishing – as if something had been suddenly lifted from the body. Immediately all the usual deductions were made for physical loss of weight, and it was discovered that there was still a full ounce of weight unaccounted for".* [2]

All five doctors took their own measurements and compared their results. Not all the patients lost the same weight, but they did lose something that could not be accounted for. Unfortunately, only four of the six patient's results could be counted due to mechanical failures or the patient dying prior to the test equipment being in place.

But what about the consistent weight loss? Everything was taken

---

[1]Jim Heddlesten, *The 21 Grams Theory*, http://www.historicmysteries.com/the-

[2] Ibid.

into account, from the air in the lungs to bodily fluids. It still could not be explained. An interesting variation occurred on the third patient, who maintained his same weight immediately upon death. But after one minute, he lost about an ounce of weight. Dr. MacDougall explained this discrepancy as follows:

*"I believe that in this case, that of a phlegmatic man slow of thought and action, that the soul remained suspended in the body after death, during the minute that elapsed before its freedom. There is no other way of accounting for it, and it is what might be expected to happen in a man of the subject's temperament".*[3]

Following the experiment and consulting with the other attending physicians, it was determined that the average weight loss of each person was ¾ of an ounce. Dr. MacDougall concluded that a human soul weighed 21 grams.

Dr. MacDougall conducted the same experiment on 15 dogs. The experiments showed no change in weight following their death. MacDougall concluded that this may signify only humans have souls.

H. LaV. Twining, a physics teacher at Los Angeles Polytechnic High School, attempted the same experiment on mice in 1917. His conclusion was in line with that of Dr. MacDougall. There was no deviation of weight when the mice died.

Dr. MacDougall was a respected physician of Haverhill and the head of the Research Society that was conducting work in this field for six years prior to the experiment. Although this experiment would be considered unethical in modern times, it is still a peculiarity that sparks a lot of criticism, ranging from the methodology used to various religious implications

Dr. MacDougall admitted that more research needed to be done, but following these experiments, Dr. MacDougall diverted his attention to obtaining the ability to photograph the soul as it left the human body. Unfortunately, following his soul weight experiments, Dr. MacDougall failed to establish any further scientific breakthroughs. Dr. Duncan MacDougal passed away in 1920.

---

[3] Ibid.

Donna Parish-Bischoff

# CHAPTER ∽3∾

KIKO

I was a toddler when I received Kiko as a gift from my Tante Mae, Tante being the German word, for Aunt. Tante Mae traveled a lot and often brought back gifts for my sibling's and me. She had traveled to Germany to her home to visit her family. This is where she found and purchased Kiko for me.

He was a baby boy doll in blue pajamas and a white bib. On the white bib was his name embroidered across the front. He had blonde hair and sky blue eyes. He had long eyelashes and had the type of eyes that would open and close. He came with batteries and if you placed him down on the ground he would walk. However with that being said, after the first round of batteries that the doll had come with died, they were never replaced, but instead removed. My family could not afford to keep replacing batteries.

One day while my dad was at work, my siblings were at school, and my mom was in the bathroom doing a hand wash in the sink. I was seated on the floor in front of the television set. From the angle I was seated at I could see straight down the long foyer leading to my bedroom. Off the foyer to the right of my bedroom was the bathroom. The bathroom door was open but the water was running so any detailed sounds were muffled.

I had been giggling at some children's show that my mother had put on the television on for me. I guess to keep my mind occupied while she did house work. I heard my mom singing aloud while she was in the bathroom. So between the water running and her singing she was not expecting what came next. I guess I was so young still and filled with magic that at first, I never thought anything of it. As you grow older these barriers are built and fears grow, but not at that moment. I was not frightened of my Kiko. I turned to see him at the end of the hallway. He only stood less than a foot tall. Not very intimidating by any measure, but there he was. Then he started to walk down the foyer towards the living room in his little robotic stance that he had. I started to laugh out loud and scream with the joy of seeing a friend, I shouted, "KIKO!"

My mother turned off the water, stopped singing and poked her head out of the bathroom door. She screamed but not in the same joyful way I was screaming. My mother ran to Kiko scooped him up. Checked for batteries, none! Then, she pulled out a black garbage bag and threw Kiko inside. She tied and knot and ran out back, and threw the bag with Kiko in the dumpster!

I cried so hard. I felt as if a friend were murdered in front of me. She ran back inside. She called my grandmother and my Tanta Mae. She explained what happened. She was shaking and pale as a ghost. I could not comprehend this entire occurrence. I was crying and screaming and angry now. My mother tried to explain to me that it was a bad thing and she had to do that.

Well, now as an adult I understand, BUT, as an adult paranormal investigator, I really wish I had that doll so I could study it or donate it to a haunted museum at this point.

Even though I know what took place that day was awfully beyond explanation, and the doll more than likely was possessed by a wandering spirit, I still miss that doll.

In 2013, I searched EBay to see if I could find another Kiko doll, and well I did, it was one hundred and thirty eight dollars. Someone in Spain was selling him. I was tempted to purchase the doll. I refrained from doing so mainly because I had an electric bill due and it just didn't seem logical to buy this doll for that kind of money.

What would you have done?

# CHAPTER ∾4∾

## TANTE MAE

Tante Mae was the first real death I had digested at the age of thirteen. She reminded me of Mrs. Claus. Yes, that "Mrs. Claus"—Of the North Pole that is.

She was a German chef. She was born and raised in Germany. She met my grandmother shortly after they both moved to America as young ladies. They lived across the street from one another on Buena Vista Avenue in Yonkers, NY. They bonded. My grandmother being from Vienna, Austria and Tante Mae being from Germany. They had a kindred ship together.

My grandmother chose Tante Mae to be everyone's God Mother. So everyone called her Tante (German for Aunt). She really was the perfect Aunt and Godmother as they come. The only thing she was missing was a magical wand, who knows maybe she had one!

She always made us feel so special when she invited us over. I remember she had an old piano in her house that she allowed me to pound on. I had no clue how to play it. I just pounded on it until I gave her an ear deafening migraine possibly, but she would never stop me. She was just overjoyed to have a child making noise in her home. When she smiled she would get this crinkle in her nose and her eyes would light up with happiness. She never had children. Always wanted to have children but couldn't have any of her own. So she borrowed us. We never minded the extra attention or love (or cookies) she would give us. I remember the day she gave me a shiny beaded change purse from one of her trips. She said look inside. There were two silver dollars and a small picture of her inside of it. Then she gave me a music box with one of those Ballerinas that twirl around when you wind it up, and inside that music box were bird shaped scented soaps. She always made me feel so special. She wanted to see the expression on my face when I opened these gift's up. I could tell it meant the world to her. She even loomed her own rugs too. She did it all.

There was one rug that still stands out in my mind until today. It was a dark navy back ground with a full yellow moon and these misty white clouds going through the moon. Just so much detail in everything she did. It went to show you she carried these details into the life she lived. At Christmas time she would bake edible ornaments! With me around they never lasted through Christmas Eve!

She would prepare these meals as if she were cooking for royalty. She would prepare these culinary spread as though Kings and Queens were visiting her. It was our family and she would make sure we had care packages to take home. I believe because she knew we did not have much and she wanted to make sure we had plenty to eat.

It always felt like a holiday if she were cooking for us. That always warmed my heart to feel that kind of love that our family had when we were together like this. Before her husband John passed away they both would fuss over me. He would cut fresh daisies and bring them in to me as I would sit at their kitchen table. She would pour me a large glass of milk and give me a plate of Oreo's. I can still see her sweet smile, her dimples as her glasses would slide to the end of her nose getting a kick out me enjoying my snack.

I remember when my mom told me when she became ill with cancer. I really did not know what cancer was or what it did to the body. I was an ignorant kid. I did not understand why Tante Mae did not recognize me anymore. I did not know about the morphine and how it makes you out of it and kills the pain.

The day she died my mom got the phone call and she told me. I felt so bad because I knew I would never get to see her again. I could not wrap my brain around this whole thing. Now I had to get a dress to see her one last time in a box. Not fair. As my mom and I parked in Chicken Island in Yonkers, a nice name for a Parking lot in Getty Square. We approached C.H. Martin's to enter the back entrance. A woman exited the store; I was in shock and in disbelief. It was my Tante Mae! Or a dead ringer for her! Holy Shit! This woman locked gazes with me and smiled. She held the door for me and said there you go sweetie. The only thing was missing was her heavy German accent. But I think it was divine intervention, call it what you may, higher power or giving me one last look at her alive smiling at me.

So although I knew she was still passed, I felt better about letting go and saying so long.

Also as a side note I found out some cool information about her. She was running a speak easy in the 1920's with her husband and running moon shine through the Palisades and kept it in the basement of his Spanish restaurant in Yonkers!

So exciting! Such a cool lady indeed to have known her and be blessed to have been loved by her for the first thirteen years of my life. Thank you, Tante Mae. I love you. Until we meet again!

Donna Parish-Bischoff

# CHAPTER ᔦ5ᔧ

## UNCLE JOHNNY

My Uncle Johnny; although I do not have too many memories of him, I can tell what I do know, from what I do remember of him, and of the day we found out he died, and I saw a part of my mom died too. It was surrealistic and something out of a weekly crime drama.

First I will tell you that from where I sat, I can tell you that Uncle Johnny loved to have a good time. He loved to laugh and loved music, dancing, good food, and he loved to joke around with my mom. My mom nicknamed him "Shorty," and he nicknamed her, "Sissy."

We would attend his house often for his yard parties; he would have barbeques, loud music. I would open endless cans of White Rock Soda, never finish them, and leave them around his house. He caught me and scorned me, shaking his finger at me with a grumpy look. I got scared and ran outside to my mother for the remainder of the night, not touching another can of White Rock soda again.

One Sunday, my mom was excited and happy that Uncle Johnny was coming over to our apartment to have dinner. She was making baked chicken and mashed potatoes with gravy. Time was going on and he was late. She had called his house and there had been no answer, but for whatever reason my mother had a deep weird feeling that something wasn't quite right. My dad rolled his eyes and threw his hand's up as he did, he said, "Oh for shit sake. Marge, stop with yer' psychic mumbo jumbo bullshit!" He probably fell asleep watching the game.

My mother was hurt by that statement. Still she had this nagging feeling something was not right. She called my grandmother to see if perhaps he stopped by her house on the way. My grandmother answered the phone and said, "No, Johnny has not been by here." Now my mother begged my dad to go over to Uncle Johnny's house to check on him.

My father picked up the car keys and sucked his teeth thinking my mother was over reacting. My mother remained at our house with me, in case Uncle Johnny would come by chance. Keep in mind the year is 1974, and there are no cell phones. You might as well use smoke signals to contact people!

Well, as my dad drove up to my Uncle's home he noticed my uncles' car in the drive way. He walked towards the back door, which was a screen door. It had been locked but my father could see into the living room. He noticed my uncle, lying on the floor in his living room. He screamed out his name, and my uncle did not move. So my father ripped the screen open, and broke into my uncles' home. It was too late, sadly my uncle was deceased. He apparently had been walking from his bedroom to the bathroom when he must have had a heart attack. At that moment, the police showed up because some neighbor witnessed my dad break into the back door.

The police questioned my father and realized there was no foul play. My mother had known within her soul that her brother was in trouble and left the physical earth. She howled and cried so hard …. I will never forget that day. I can still hear her in my head. I got so upset for her, that I remember puking up uncontrollably. My brother had to clean me up and make sure I was okay.

I had never been to a funeral before and so they tried to keep me downstairs in the waiting area. My sister and brother would take turns occupying me as my mom would be in the viewing room. It was my sister's turn. She said, "I have to go to the bathroom, come with me." I was seven, and she did not want me to get kidnapped. So while she was in one of the stalls doing her business, I asked her for a dime. She really did not think twice about it.

She slid a dime out from under the stall and here. I placed the dime in what I thought was a toy dispenser. I was bored from being kept downstairs away from people. I missed my mother; I wanted to cheer her up. Before my sister could finish up, I was out the door with my new toy skipping up the carpeted funeral steps. Pushing through the crowd of all my relatives swinging my toy around by its string. I said, "Look Ma! They sell toys downstairs for a dime!"

Yes, I did that in the viewing room none the less! My mother wanted to faint. She grabbed her mouth and said, "Where is your Sister?" My brother quickly grabbed the tampon out of my hand and wrangled me like a loose wild boar at a rodeo. My sister came upstairs unaware of what I had done and looking for me. My mother was so angry at Doreen for giving me that dime. She said, "You knew NO good could have come from that!" Poor Doreen had no idea! I was hard to handle and had no clue what the hell it was. To my defense it was a toy with a string.

But I guess the whole point of this chapter is that my mother knew

24

that her brother had left this world. She and all of her siblings were so close that they all knew when the other was hurting or sick, or even when they passed. Where there is love, there are no boundaries.

Donna Parish-Bischoff

# CHAPTER ∿6∿

FIRST STREET, YONKERS, NY. 1979

This story picks up where life left us after Lee Avenue. My family and I just had a reprieve from a five year sentence of one of the most terrifying experiences that changed the way I looked at life, and the thereafter forever. Not only did we have this paranormal entity and life changes, but we also we faced ridicule from our neighbors and our local Parish.

So maybe this move was a healthy, fresh start. My dad was headed back to work after his long battle from suffering a heart attack and open-heart surgery. My brother had graduated college and was now working for Fuji in Scarsdale. My sister was happily working at the Board of Education. I was entering that awkward stage where a twelve year old has acne, thick eyeglasses, hairy legs, chubby, and no one understood me.

But something else was also shifting inside me as well; that era of adolescence where the veil to the earthly and the unearthly are like Plexiglas and now visible to someone of my nature. My mom was again determined to make this place home for all of us.

She had obtained a large quantity of a beautiful upholstery material. It was white and deep royal blue, with a floral pattern (but not tacky looking). She fired up her antique Singer sewing machine and while everyone was out during the day, she started making matching slipcovers and drapes. She even made throw pillows too! Everything came out just beautiful, and looking so professional.

I shared a room with my sister again, my brother had his own room, and my parents had the pull out sofa bed. It was the first time in five years we were all beginning to feel normal again. Everyone seemed to be doing their own thing and life had its rhythm.

Within a year of living at First Street, my brother's job offered him a promotion and he was asked to move to Japan for about a year. My sister started to stay over at her friend's houses more often, and going away on the weekends.  My dad kept picking up extra hours to work.

So now, it was mostly just me and my mom.  It was only then when I started to notice, little by little, small things occur. Because of Lee Avenue, I wasn't sure if it was my mind playing games with me. I thought maybe I was having residual thoughts. But these things were different than what happened on Lee Avenue. It's almost as though they wanted to capture your attention —not hurt you, or scare you. But once it did. It would stop or go away.

I knew I needed to follow this path because the story was clearly not over by a long shot.  Spirits were letting me know they were present.

# CHAPTER ∽7∾

## LET ME TELL YOU ABOUT
## "MY BEST FRIEND"

It was 1981, when I met Donna. I was thirteen, and she was fourteen. We instantly connected. It felt like to me that we had a connection that had continued, not one that had just began. We knew a lot about Donna's experiences with the paranormal because she would share her stories with us. Even though she made all of us a little scared, we still enjoyed hearing these stories.

Never once, did my gut ever tell me that she was deceiving us in any way. We all believed her. Having always trusted Donna, even though I, had never seen, heard, felt, or known a true real-life paranormal experience, I was open to the fact that it did exist, until this one night at Donna's.

Donna asked her mom if it would be okay if me, my sister Anita, and our friend Rose, could sleep over. Mrs. Parish said, "Sure." My sister, Anita, is three years older than me, and our friend Rose, is the same age. So Rose and I were thirteen at the time. This is the night I experienced first-hand, along with my sister, what Donna had been telling me all about. As far as Rose, she fell asleep on the living room couch, watching MTV, missing the entire event!

Donna's brother had moved out and gave her his bedroom. She had it painted Pepto-Bismol pink (some call it Drunk Tank Pink). She had made it more of a sitting, music room with a desk, stereo and a couch. We were listening to 'The Police' on her record player. We kept the door to the room open.

There was a corner chair Donna had by the door, and my sister Anita decided to "get a little cocky" and mock the unseen. She wanted to see if the spirit would respond to her. She said, "Can I sit in that chair?" Donna said, "But what if the ghost is sitting in that chair?" Anita began to sit down in the chair and said, "OK if you are here I will sit in your lap."

At that moment, Anita sat down in that chair and at that exact moment the door slammed shut, the lights went out and the music stopped. The door had even locked itself. I had been sitting on the couch, Donna had been standing. The three of us scrambled, screaming, and banging into each other like the three stooges! Mrs. Parish heard us in hysterics, and came running down the long hallway from the kitchen. The door suddenly unlocked, the lights came on, the three of us were huffing and puffing, eyes wide with fear. Rose still in slumber land on the living room couch, sleeping through the whole ordeal.

That was the night we became a part of that elite club.

Story Submitted by: Beth Schwartz-Abrams, Yonkers, New York

# CHAPTER ∽8∾

## PEARLS OF WISDOM

One day after school I walked home to Donna's house. This was the same house where I had my first experience with the door slamming shut, and the light's shutting off on us girls. I will never forget that night.

Donna and I were going to do our homework together then go get pizza out on Mclean Avenue. As we entered her apartment, she said come here I want to show you some stuff we found. She led me down a long flight of steep stairs to a semi-finished basement. I followed Donna down the stairs and she walked over to a box of belongings that was left behind by the previous owners.

There was the normal stuff, some clothes, shoes, until she pulled out this beautiful egg white colored pearl. Donna looked up at me and started to tell me that rumor had it that the previous owner had died on the front steps of the apartment of a heart attack, and these were his and his wife's ' belongings.

Donna offered the pearl to me because I admired it. It seemed harmless enough. Well, let's say I found out the hard way that some spirits don't like when you have their material belongings. From the first night of having this pearl in my possession anything that could have gone, did go wrong. A string of bad luck. Nothing would prepare me for what I would find when I awoke the very next morning.

Two major thing's happened to me that morning. The first thing was as soon as I opened my eyes I noticed my Sylvester Stallone poster that was hanging above my bed had been decapitated. It was cut in two! I naturally asked my sister if perhaps she did this as a sick joke but she swore she did not! I knew she didn't deep inside but I had to ask. I asked my parent's and they was as shocked as I was looking it, they had no idea what could of transpired. Okay, if they did not do that and I would never do that how did this happen and by whom?

It was not torn. It was cut clearly with a scissor, a clean cut too! So

31

weird! I knew I had to get ready for school and I was not going to get any answers this strange occurrence that took place. I was standing in the bathroom with the door wide open and I can see clear into the dining area and part of the kitchen behind me. I was blow drying my hair and looking into the mirror. I could see part of the kitchen behind me. I was blow drying my hair and looking into the mirror. As I glanced past my face and into the dining room behind me I suddenly noticed a heavy set, middle aged, and red headed woman, seated in my father's captain's chair with a very angry expression on her face. She was as solid as looking at a real person. She was just leering at me with discontent. I turned around so fast to see who got into the apartment with me, and she was no longer there.

I rushed to get my stuff together for school; I did not want to be late. I knew I needed to tell Donna what was happening. I took the pearl with me. Meeting Donna at the lockers, I asked her to follow me into the bathroom so I could tell her what I had just been through this morning. We hurried into the bathroom and I began to tell Donna the entire ordeal when one of the bathroom stalls opened up and it, and it was our other friend, Jackie. She overheard what I had said about the pearl and all the bad luck and that woman I saw through my bathroom mirror.

Jackie held out her hand and offered to take the pearl. She said: "Let me see if anything happens while in my possession." We both raised our eyebrows at her as if to say, "REALLY?"

She took the pearl and stuffed it in the back pocket of her jeans. She said, "I will keep you posted," and smiled. Well, we didn't hear or see from Jackie for about five days after offering to take the pearl. She met up with us at school and said she flushed that "fuckin' thing down the toilet and she was sorry if I was upset. I said no not at all and asked, "Why? What happened?" She said she got into fights; she had failed a test and fell since she took it. It had a bad vibe and it had to go!

It was obvious that something bad was attached to that pearl! This entity, spirit, call it what you will wanted no one to have this pearl. This was one lesson we will never forget.

Submitted by Beth Abrams Yonkers, New York and Jackie Axt , Congers , New York

# CHAPTER ❧9❧

### GOODBYE MOM, WITH LOVE

Whoever has lost a mom knows what this is like. It feels as if your soul was ripped from your body. You feel like a lost kid at an airport, and no one will ever come to find you again.

My mom was my best friend. She was that person that I could stay up late at night with, drinking coffee or tea in the kitchen. We would giggle our heads off at stupid things. She understood me like no one could. She loved me in spite of myself and didn't care that I was weird. She was everyone's mom. My friends loved her gooey grill cheese sandwiches and hot tea. She would put headphones on from the Walkman and dance about to the Rolling Stones, Brown Sugar, but yet she was a lady, and had a great sense of humor. We had shitty health care coverage and hardly enough money to cover the rent and bills. She suffered in silence most of the time, and we never knew it. Looking back, I could kick myself now, but I know my mom would not want me to do that. I can almost hear her say, "That would be in vain."

One day my Aunty Anna and Aunt Mame were visiting from Pine Plains. Before they left they grabbed her face to kiss her goodbye, and they pulled back in extreme shock. My sister and I looked on in disbelief as well. How did we never see this, and how had my mother kept this hidden. Apparently she had hidden, two huge lumps behind her ears, with her hair for months.

She said she didn't want to bother anyone. Well, needless to say, the following months were racing her to get Chemo and radiations were in vain. She was diagnosed with stage four non-Hodgkin's lymphoma. I was twenty-one years old and I was losing my best friend. I suppose it seems old enough to be on my own, but my heart was breaking. This was my mommy.

I was not the only one who was losing her. Of course there was my sister, my brother, my dad, and her other siblings. This did not have to be. Something could have been done to prevent this. Why did she choose this? I tortured myself emotionally with the whys and what ifs. I was a lost soul.

I held her hand and I never cried in front of her. She called me her brave soldier. So I needed to be just that. I would bring her Hazelnut coffee in a thermos to the hospital when she could hold it down. I brought a manicure kit so I could do her nails because that is what we did at home. We did our nails! I did her make up.

I turned on the chapel channel in that broadcasted directly from the hospital's chapel, which was located downstairs. I told my mom, "Keep watching mom—I will be on TV!" I would run downstairs and into the chapel; then I would go in front of the camera and make faces at her to make her laugh. OK, so not wise of me, BUT she liked it, then I would race back up before the nuns could catch me!

I did my best not to cry in front of her. Then that day came. It was a Tuesday night around 10pm. She waited until we all left. She refused to go when we were all there. Stubborn as usual! I finally let it all go.

She passed away October 27, 1992. I remember there being this whole big-to-do over having the actual burial on October 31. I begged them not to because I know my mother was superstitious about Halloween and did not want to get stuck in-between the two worlds forever. So we buried her on the 30th. I did not attend the wake session the first night. I just couldn't. I saw the blue dress they picked for her as if it were a ball she was attending. It was pretty and all. I saw the brown wig that my aunt had bought for her before she passed. She did trim it somewhat the way my mom had her hair, but a wig is a wig. I just couldn't see my mom, looking like that, in a box.

I wanted to remember her alive and smiling, plain and simple. I did manage to attend the next night, it was the last night of the wake. I stayed to the back and glanced over to the casket. She wasn't my mother any longer. I went downstairs to the lounge area and I sat with my friends. I cried, then we laughed at the fun times, then I cried some more.

Then the reality hit again. The stupid roller coaster of death rocked me and threw me deeper than I ever felt before. It was nine o'clock, the parlor had been emptied out, and echoes of "I'm so sorry," rang inside my head for days. I was numb and angry. I was lost and empty. I was faithless, and I felt hollow.

On November 3, around 10pm, I was alone in the house. My dad had gone to the Vet's lodge to play cards and feel less alone. My sister and her husband were in their basement apartment sleeping. I had been sitting on my bed on the phone. My cat La La Berry had run into the bedroom and mewed, standing up holding one paw out, like she was doing stupid pet trick. She was facing the corner of my bedroom. This corner was my mom's favorite part of my room. I had big balloon curtains, a round table, and two wrought iron bistro chairs facing the park. She called it her "French corner, her "Shangri-La."

Just then, I stopped speaking on the phone. I noticed something quite extraordinary. A brilliant orb of light that cannot be duplicated by artificial lighting and verbally describing it would do it no justice. This ball of light became so bright and large and took the shape of a person standing there. La La Berry tried to touch it, and did not run. My mom LOVED that cat so much and La La loved my mom. I dropped the phone. I had no time to react. It was over within seconds. There was no sound.

To this day, I even forget who the hell I was on the phone with! I think the light that night was my mother saying, "So long and do not lose faith." And so because of that night I have not. It was powerful, more powerful than any other single, experience I have ever encountered in my life. Never lose faith, just believe, and know they are there.

So long for now mom, with love, see you soon. Your soldier, Donna.

Donna Parish-Bischoff

# CHAPTER ❧10❧

### THE BOX

Before my mother passed away she had decided to go through all the years of papers, and card's from my sibling's, and myself, to her. She went through our homemade cards to her, drawing's from school and home, and she marked each box, with each of our names on it.

I came home from work and went up to my room. There on my bed was the "Donna Box". It was filled with everything I ever gave her or made her in it. I went downstairs for dinner and sat down. I asked her about it. She said quite simply enough "When I am gone I don't want you fretting or wondering or worrying about having to go through everything yourself."

In this box she kept some art work of mine that she cherished and gave her hope out of everything. Yes it was childish and crazy looking BUT there were two special reasons why it gave her hope. I started drawing these figures and wrote the word "Heaven "in each picture, shortly after I had an allergic reaction to a measles vaccination that made me stop breathing and I turned blue. My mother had to administer CPR and call for help before I came to after ten or fifteen minutes. She said I was lifeless like a rag doll, and blue. But I had a fascination for heaven after that.

I cannot tell you much myself. I do not remember any bright lights or angels. I do not. I won't lie. But I do remember my odd fascination with heaven as a little girl. So for that alone I guess I was connected with some invisible umbilical cord. I haven't quite figured it all out if much out just yet. As we all know we learn as we go. If anyone tells you they are an expert out there, RUN!

Here are those images I drew so long ago. I miss my mom so much but sometimes I make a pot of coffee and look through that box of cards and pictures and I know and feel she is right next to me.

HEAVEN

Donna Parish-Bischoff

# CHAPTER ✑11✑

### THE GHOST OF CHRISTMAS PAST

It was the second Christmas after my mom had passed; the year was 1992. After she passed away we moved out of the home we had all gathered together for several holidays. It was hard to live there anymore with empty rooms and memories of what once was. It was time for our family to move on and carry our mother in hearts and make new memories in a new place.

My dad and I split the rent, and shared a duplex apartment in a two family home in a quiet suburban neighborhood of Yonkers, NY. My sister and her husband found a lovely apartment closer to their jobs. And my brother and his wife remained in Long Island, and would continue visiting us from time to time.

Being that Christmas was nearing, I wanted to make it a happier memory for all of us. The year before was still raw, and weeks after her death. We did not celebrate. It was depressing and somber. Christmas always meant so much to my mom, my dad too. But I knew my dad was still feeling down. For without my mom there getting the ball rolling, his heart wasn't in it.

I ordered up a nine foot artificial tree through an online catalog. I bought large and small sparkly plastic snowflakes and invisible string to hang them from the ceiling. I love cooking and baking so I planned a big meal and desserts. I just wanted to turn things around for us. I know it was different. It would NEVER be the same without mom. She was our glue. She made holidays special. But I had to try to jump start something.

I had stopped in a local store up the block, and found a really pretty frame. It was made of ceramic and it had these battery operated holiday lights on it that would only light up IF you pushed a button in the front, and those lights would ONLY stay on for about ten seconds, then stop until you pushed the button again. I decided it would be a nice conversation piece to place a family picture in. One that had my mother in it of course, and place it on the corner lamp table next to the couch in the living room.

I went to town in the next few days decorating, and preparing for Christmas Day, and our family visit. I was excited. I had the radio on in the kitchen as I cooked and baked playing Christmas music to get me in the mood. I had lights strung up in our front windows. Maybe I over did it a bit but I will always remember that Christmas in my heart.

The day had arrived and it was around ten o'clock in the morning when my sister and her husband, and my brother and his wife had arrived. The coffee was up and my dad had his Lincoln Park Bakery rolls on the table. Those were a staple in our home as far back as I can remember. They were delicious.

There was this void in all of our eyes, our hearts and souls. No amount of sparkly snowflakes or wonderfully wrapped gift would lift that sadness of not having mom there to share it with us.

But like that song suggests, "Until then, we'll just have to muddle through somehow, and have ourselves a merry little Christmas now."

Our gift was in the here and now with each other. Our laughter. Our dad's corny jokes! And, OH Boy were they ever corny! Slowly as the day was coming to a close and the meals were finished and gifts were unwrapped and bagged and ready to go home. The table was cleared. Dishes were being washed. My sister helped me tidy up and little by little everyone said their goodbyes until the next family visit. Very bittersweet.

Then it was me and my dad. I could tell he was holding back a tear. Biting his lip. But he would rather not be known for having too much of a soft side. So he said smiled and thanked me for a lovely Christmas and told me he was headed to bed. I said, "Sure Dad, good night."

Then it was me. In this silent house. Wow. So weird. After all this preparation. The hype. The buildup. Now poof! Over! I went into the living room to unplug the window lights, tree lights, etc. as I flipped the wall plate switch off to shut off the overhead ceiling light. The living room was dark. Something caught the corner of my eye. I did a double take and ran back into the living room. It was the picture frame blinking away at me! As I approached it had stopped! I was nowhere near it. I did not press its button to make it go. You had to physically push hard on the front button to make it blink. I became teary eyed and smiled. I looked around and said, "Merry Christmas Mom! I Love You Too!"

# CHAPTER ❧12❧

## MA' BELL CALLING

My dad overcame many obstacles in his lifetime. He was struck with Polio in the early 1930's, and could not walk for a period of time. His dad used a variety of diversified techniques on him as therapy until he finally started to walk again. Let's just say they were unconventional and leave it at that.

His childhood was hard, as he and his two siblings' often had to listen to the adults argue in French so they wouldn't figure out what they were fighting about. Then one day my dad's mother left the kid's with their dad and grandmother. That left my aunt to be the second mother to her older brothers. As my dad grew older, he joined the army, and fought in the Korean War. He hated to speak about the unmentionable things he had to do at times, during the war. When watching war movies, he would tear up a lot. He had a gruff exterior, and always had a rough and tumble attitude, where you always thought you did something wrong. It was just the way he was raised. He was misunderstood and left behind. I didn't get that when I was a kid. He was like this 10,000 piece puzzle to me. It wasn't until after he died when I put all the pieces together. It was too late by that time. Regretfully so.

The last four years of his life we shared a duplex apartment together, and it was only during the last two years of his life, that we did actually bond, and become friends. We both worked during the week so we really only saw each other on a Sunday. He would run out to Lincoln Park Bakery, down on Mclean Avenue. They had the most amazing rolls. My dad would make a fresh pot of coffee, and we would sit, and enjoy these rolls still warm from the bakery oven. We would catch up for about an hour, before we started our day.

Sometimes dad would go out and shoot golf balls, or hang out at the Veterans Post 1666, where he was the Commander for several terms. He was also the director of the Veterans Hospital in Kingsbridge, Bronx. So he would spend much of his time helping other Vets getting what they needed.

It was about two weeks before my dad died, (I had no idea he was dying), that I told him, "I never thought you liked me dad." He began to tear up, and he put his hands in his pockets. He looked down and began to tear up again, then, he said, "I'm sorry. I never meant to make you feel that way." He said he loved me and was proud of me. I felt bad for even telling him that. I told him I was glad to finally be honest with him, and I said I was happy that we had become good friends.

As I grew older I realized I am a lot like my dad. I don't take shit from anyone. I am as cuddly as a cactus, but I mean well. When my dad worked for City Hall under Mayor Zaleski, he declared June 20th, George Parish Day. In the Proclamation he nicknamed my dad "Pit-bull Parish," because my dad never let anything go. My dad fought for his causes until he got his way. Well, I like to think of myself in somewhat of the same way, and I am proud of that I am like my father.

About a week before he passed away, on a Saturday morning around 10AM, I was upstairs cleaning my area of the apartment first when he called for me from the bottom of the stairway. I came down and said, "What's up dad?" He looked frightened. I said, "What's the matter?" He asked me the weirdest question. He asked me if we had an earthquake or a severe thunderstorm the night before. I said, "Noooooo, why?" He said, "Something was shaking my bed all night. I was afraid to leave the room."

Okay, for my dad to be fearful of ANYTHING or admit to being fearful of ANYTHING, was BIG! I did not have a good feeling about it, but I could see he was shitting pickles, grapes, and cannon balls so I played it off, and said, "Maybe you had a nightmare dad!", and started laughing. I knew that if he saw I laughed it off, he would relax.

He suddenly looked at me and said, "Oh yeah, maybe you're right. I probably did." He started to laugh nervously and said, "I'm an Asshole! Ha Ha Ha!" I said, "NO, you're not. Dreams can seem real at times dad," but I really did not have a good feeling. I mean this was my dad who had shit fly around under his nose on Lee Avenue, and he claimed nothing! So, this was epic for me.

One week later, I was making homemade soup, and I forgot stewed tomatoes. My dad said he wanted to lay down, he wasn't feeling well. I said I would be back in ten minutes. I went to Stop & Shop around the corner. I came back and I heard him in his room. He was in distress, moaning. I walked in and he was sitting up, and there he was throwing up, blood on his shirt. I called 911, then my brother, then my sister. We all rushed to Saint Joseph's Hospital in Yonkers. That was November

14<sup>th</sup>. He was gone by November 17<sup>th</sup>.

They said it was acute pancreatitis. A month earlier the two of us were pumpkin picking with Larry, Gerry, and my two year old niece. He was all smiles and we were laughing. What the fuck was happening?

A couple of month's passed, and I moved into my own apartment because there was no way I could keep up with paying the entire rent for the duplex my dad and I shared. Plus, even if I could afford it, I didn't want to stay there remembering what took place.

So here I was in my new place. It was a fresh start out on my own totally. I had one bedroom apartment. It was "cozy" as the realtor' called it (code word, small), but perfect for me. I didn't need much. It had a kitchen, a small living room, and the bedroom was actually large. I slowly worked on making it my own.

I missed my dad, our Sunday coffee catch-up talks, and our Lincoln Park Bakery rolls. My life will never be the same again. Both my parents were gone. I was officially on my own. It felt so strange not to be able to call them, or talk to them on the drop of a dime. It was weird to wake up to a silent apartment. No noises or hearing dishes and utensils were being washed in the sink, or low voices mumbling in conversation. It was just me and of course my cat, La La Berry.

One night I went to bed like I did every other night, nothing out of the ordinary. I always kept the over the stove light on. It would shine like a night light through the small apartment. It was helpful so I would not break my neck getting to the bathroom in the middle of the night. I got up the next day and awoke from a very vivid dream of my dad. I was glad to see him, but I thought it was odd. I dreamt he was at my job, seated next to my desk, dressed in a white button down shirt, and his grey dress pants. He had his legs crossed, and he was wearing his reader glasses at the edge of his nose. He was holding his Herald Statesman newspaper. He leaned forward, and folded the paper down. He said to me, "Donna pay your fuckin' phone bill," then, poof, I woke up. I thought, "Oh boy, how nuts was that dream?"

I shook it off and kinda laughed at it. Leave it to dad to yell at me in my dreams about my bills! Growing up he was always shutting off the lights if you left the room even for a second. You could hear him yell "I ain't Fuckin' Con Ed God Dammit!" It was hard for us money wise, but when you're a kid you don't get that. You grow up and boy oh boy you learn it fast!

So that morning I scrambled to get to work on time, fed La La Berry, grabbed my lunch, car keys and I was off and running. My work day became busy and my dream left my immediate memory for moment. I really didn't have a second thought about it to be honest. It was five o'clock, quitting time and I was glad to be getting out of work. I stopped at A&P on the way home to pick up some dinner for myself, and some cat food for La La Berry, and then I proceeded home.

As I drove home, the dream popped back into my head and I began to chuckle and I shook my head as to say "Only dad." I pulled up to my apartment and parked. I made my way up the cement steps and to the wooden porch. I reached into the mail slot with my name on it. I pulled out a pile of mail but with dim lighting, I could not see what was what until I got into the apartment. I slipped my key into the cylinder and unlocked my door, letting myself in. I flipped the kitchen light switch on, and threw the mail onto the counter. I placed the grocery bags on the table and took off my coat. I went back to the pile of mail.

Flipping through the envelopes, I stopped dead in my tracks! Whoa! It was my phone bill! Dad did tell me to pay it! A chill went up my spine at that minute, and I began to laugh. I said, "I got it dad!" Talk about your long distance calls! I will never forget that dream or visit—never.

# CHAPTER ❦13❧

## A CHANGE OF CLOTHES, A CHANGE OF SPIRIT

It wasn't too long after the last dream of my dad about the phone bill that I had another dream of my dad. This one seemed to pack more of a symbolic resonance to it this time. I was in front of an old white Victorian home modest in style. The door was open. It appeared to be warm weather. Not hot or cold—just comfortable. A lovely staircase covered with red oriental carpeting led to a second floor. I entered the home and walked into the living room or sitting area of some form. The place was quiet. There was not a soul around. I heard my father's throat clear as he did when he was alive. He had a very distinctive sound. I called out, "Dad?" I saw a man coming from the back room buttoning up a white shirt and it appeared to be my dad, but in his late twenties— maybe early thirties. He had dark curly hair and tanned skin. I could see his bright green eyes.

He spoke clear as day and said, "Donna, I am changing spirits now." I believe this was my dad telling me he was crossing over and was at peace with the thing's that kept him earthbound. It was a wonderful gift to see and hear this from him. Thank you dad for letting me know you got there safely.

I looked up what this dream may have meant, and I found out that when you dream of the dead living and happy, this signifies that you are letting the wrong influences into your life, which will bring material loss if not corrected. A young woman dreaming of an authority figure or her father signifies that her lover is playing her false.

I do believe that I was communicating with my father's spirit on some level. The interesting factor regarding this analysis is, at the time of his death, I was ending a very long and tulmulchious relationship. I know he would very happy to know I was no longer in that relationship.

Seeing a staircase in your dream symbolizes change and transformation. Going up and down a staircase can represent a rise or fall in economic or social status and lack the general efforts that are required to accomplish life's small and large goals. To see a staircase in your dream symbolizes change and transformation.

I believe the deceased come to us in our dreams and show us symbols in order to help us figure a problem out. I think my dad was coming to me to help me out of a potentially harmful situation.

# CHAPTER ❧14❧

## BEAR MOUNTAIN NATIVE AMERICAN

It was late August of 1997. It was the night of a full moon. I had been in a relationship with a man ten years my senior. We had gotten together just before my mother passed away. At first everything seemed wonderful and perfect. By this point, we had been together almost eight years, but there had been an obvious strain on the relationship. There was stagnancy, sadness, and a block. I felt as if we couldn't move forward and yet we couldn't end this cycle. What began as a great friendship, a great romance of sorts, at some point had turned into a dying plant, left behind, in an abandoned office building.

Oddly enough, we were still in the habit to be in each other's company, and be miserable with one another. I called "Alvin" around seven in the evening and asked if he wanted me to pick him up to drive up to Bear Mountain to watch the full moon rise. He said, "Sure." So, I drove across town to get him arriving about seven forty- five. He came out and seemed out of it and a little depressed. At the time, I had an old Volkswagen Jetta 4-seater, with a sunroof. He was tall and lanky, so he had to push the seat as far back as possible.

I asked him what was the matter and he was just mumbling and sulking and that always pissed me off because I felt if he didn't want to come out then he should have stayed home. So that got me into a bitchy mood. Then of course the bickering began between us. He started in about the way I drove. It festered into a bunch of unhealthy topics for seemingly, adult people.

As I made my way up to Bear Mountain our bickering became unbearable, no pun intended. My heart felt heavy with great sadness. I felt lost. I finally pulled into the parking lot of the Bear Mountain Lodge. I said to Alvin, "I have to use the restroom, I will be right back." He remained in the car. I entered the lodge and it was quiet, no one was inside. It was closer to nine o'clock by this time. I made my way to the ladies room. There was not a soul in there. I closed the stall door behind me and started to do my business.

Out of nowhere I begin to hear this angelic singing. Unlike anything I have ever heard. It sounded Native American to me. It was so beautiful I felt my eyes well up with water from the beauty of it. I truly cannot find words to express the beauty that I felt at that moment. Tears just streamed from my eyes. It touched me in a way that I cannot possibly tell you.

I finished up and left the stall. I followed the music out of the ladies room. It was not in the lodge. I followed it outside. I discovered right on the lawn of Bear Mountain there appeared a Native American gentleman in full headdress and he was wearing all black clothes. He wore feathered earrings. He resembled Johnny Cash in a weird way to me.

He was doing tai chi while facing the mountains and the full moon as he listened to his music. I walked up to him feeling a little nervous. He turned to me and smiled. I said, "Excuse me." I smiled and said "Hello." I said, "I hate to bother you, but what is this music you're listening to? I heard it from inside the lodge and I really love it." He said it was the sound track from *How the West Was Lost*. I said thank you and I began to walk away. He said wait a minute. I said, "Yes." He said, "Everything comes to an end." I said, "Excuse me?" Because of the way I had been feeling, I felt a little caught off guard by this statement. He said, "When you bang your fingernail, it turns black, and it falls off. You grow another, fresh, new fingernail. Like your relationship will end over there (as he pointed towards my car). It will be alright. You will be okay miss," he insisted as he looked at me in a meditative stance. I was scared of my future but I felt better about it.

I started to tear up and I felt that you could have blown me over with one of his feather earrings! I really believe I was meant to be there that night to hear that music, to find that Indian and to get that message because not all of our angels are in the spirit world. I believe they are breathing and living amongst us and they are here giving us messages. We just need to be at the right place at the time to receive these messages.

As I went back to the car "Alvin" asked what the whole thing was about and I told him I wanted to know about the music. I left the rest of the message out. That message was meant for me. Needless to say, and oddly enough, about two weeks later, "Alvin" broke things off with me to be with a woman who he met at his new job. Thanks to my Native American Angel, I was okay with that. He prepared me for this toenail that fell off! I shall never forget that man that night at Bear Mountain. He changed my life.

# CHAPTER ❧15❧

THE COOK AVENUE ENCOUNTERS

<u>Beulah</u>

It was my very first apartment on my own. I was thirty-one years old. My father had passed away one month prior. It was December 26th, 1998. It was a bitterly, cold day. My brother and I moved my stuff, back and forth, in a U-Haul, about ten times before we done! My life was moved in a matter of hours, my dad's belongings were divided up amongst Larry, Doreen, and me. The rest were taken to Montrose.

By five o'clock, I was all moved in, and everyone was gone. I was in a sea of boxes, and it was just me and La La Berry, my cat. It felt strange and lonely. I knew it would take some getting used to. This was the first time I had lived alone. I know I was more than old enough to be on my own, but I was always surrounded by family. So it was different to not have someone, some sort of noise, or someone talking in the back drop, or calling out to me or vice versa.

So, I unpacked my kitchen boxes first, and found my coffee maker, and put up a pot of coffee so I could keep myself going through the night, to unpack, and settle in as much as possible. I made sure I set up La La Berry's cat bed and bowls, so the both of us could start to relax a bit. The apartment began to smell like a cozy home with the coffee aroma wafting through the rooms. La La Berry was nervously crawling low, slowly, inspecting our new place together.

I found the bed sheets and the pillows and set them aside to make the bed. I went back to the kitchen to pour the coffee when I heard the strangest thing. It made me jump. I actually made a weird screeching sound and grabbed my mouth. I heard a very loud, deep-voiced woman almost growling say. "Demons and whores! Witches, Demons, and Whores!", then, more garbled growling.

I put my head to the floor of my apartment, and realized it was coming from the basement apartment. The noises stopped after ten minutes, but it was unsettling, to say the least. I did not hear anyone else speaking. I did not hear a radio or TV. Just the growling.

I called my landlady, who lived directly across the street. Her name was Nina. I asked, "Who the heck is living in the basement?" She started to laugh, she said, "Oh, I see you met Beulah." I said, "No not really. I hear her though." I told her exactly what I heard. She acted as though she had no idea what I was speaking about.

Then she confessed to me that Beulah had lived there for over twenty years, she was on a fixed income. Had no family. They felt bad for her. She was a shut in. They brought her food and things she needed. She was different. I said, "I'll say," and then I hung up.

One day, I went to take my garbage out, and she jumped out of her apartment like a beast, grabbing my garbage bag away from me, and dragged it into her apartment. I shouted, "Hey! Don't do that! That's garbage!" I complained to the landlady that in addition to things I don't want to mention, I also throw away cat litter. The land lady said not to worry, that Beulah would throw out what she would not use. I was so grossed out by this troubled woman. And frightened!

It was around 1:00AM on a Saturday morning, I had just settled into bed I could see the reflection of the stove light shine through from the kitchen into my bedroom. La La Berry was curled up beside me on the bed, and I rested my hand across her back for security. I felt my body slowly drifting off into slumber. All of a sudden, I heard Beulah growling and screaming, "Demons are here! Demons are here! You're gonna burn in hell! You witch! You're gonna burn in hell! You whore!"

I jumped up and said, "Fuck this!" I did not care that it was 1AM in the morning! I called Nina. I said, "Get over here now and tell Beulah to shut up! I can't take it." Of course, Nina took her sweet ass time to come across the street. And of course, Beulah, was all 'Demon and Witched out' by the time Nina got there!

Later that year, I had started dating my now husband and he had ended up moving in. I had warned him of Beulah and her outbursts. He actually heard her many nights as we spoke on the phone for hours. I would hold the phone to the floor and he could hear her crystal clear! I now knew the reason why the last tenant had moved out!

Flash forward to springtime. John was sitting on the couch watching TV and I was at the computer reading e-mails. We kept hearing Beulah screaming and going on and on. I remember it was a couple of days before Easter because I was making baskets for John's nephews, and his niece. I picked up the phone shook my head and said, "Enough is enough already! I am calling Nina over to hear this shit! " Nina picked up the phone and I said, "Nina you have to get over here right away." She said, "Why Donna?" I said, "I can't take it! It's Beulah again. She won't shut up!" Nina said in a sarcastic tone, "I really find that hard to believe." I said, "Really, and why is that? " Nina answered, "Because she died two weeks ago Donna and she is sitting in the morgue unclaimed!"

I dropped the damned phone! I said, "WHAT!! No! That can't be!" I picked the phone up. I said, "Nina, is this a joke? John and I are hearing her go on and on down there yelling and screaming." Nina said, "It is not a joke. No one ever claimed her body."

So now, I look like the nut job to my land lady! Great! Gheesh!

Looking back, I feel bad for Beulah. Really, she was a tortured soul. No one came around for her ever. Just a food drop off. Her life consisted of rummaging through garbage and hallucinating about demons and witches.

Was she hallucinating or warning us? You know, after I found out she died, we never heard her again. May her soul rest in Peace.

## The Dark Man

I have witnessed so many unworldly and unexplainable situations that no matter how long I sit here trying to figure it out, I would never be able to do it. So instead, all I can do is share the experiences with all of you, and hope that someday, on some level, they will make sense.

Some of these things happened before I met my current husband. Some of them happened after, and they even interacted with him. I will share all of them with you.

The apartment I lived in was once a house that was a one family home. It was now broken into a three family, apartment building. If I had to guess the circa of the era of the house, it would be around the 1920's. The DiBello family; the parents of Nina and Cassy, my landladies, owned the house.

Their dad was once a Yonkers politician; he was now deceased. Growing up, I remember my dad mentioning him. When I moved in, I remember asking who had the apartment before me. They told me the previous tenant was a nurse named Michelle, who had a cat, and that her cat had passed away. I did not think too much beyond that. They said there was a young couple above me with a newborn, and that at the time we were the only ones in the building.

I was working many overtime hours to save up for a computer and a desk set for my apartment. I finally ordered my computer and I went to pick up my desk and chair from a local office supply store. I spent my entire day off putting the desk together, then hooking the computer up to a dial-up internet service provider. Those were the good ole days! It sounded like Morse code every time I wanted to get online to check my e-mail! I finally set my desk up with my Lava lamp, and my Wiccan day planner. I would make a pot of coffee, and spend hours online, chatting, checking e-mails, all before this Face- thingy came about. So in case you didn't know, e-mail is how one got in touch with friends in the 90's!

As I recall, it was about 11PM, on a Friday night. I was getting pretty tired, so I shut down the computer, and got into bed. It must have been around 3AM or so when I awoke out of a dead sleep hearing a man calling out my name, *Donna*. I sat up in bed and said in a very annoyed voice shouted, "WHAT?"

I looked at the area where my computer was and I noticed a man with dark wavy hair, beige pants, a dark shirt, and sweater vest on. He was leaning up against the computer desk and he had his arms crossed in front, with his head tilted. Just that quickly, he vanished. He looked familiar to me, as if I knew him; yet I know I have never seen him before and I have never seen him since.

For him to be so loud and physically visual to me, it was clear to me this spirit was strong, and had some kind of a connection to me. I have always thought about that person, wondered who they were, and what they wanted.

I don't know how, but I was able to get back to sleep that night. I did not feel frightened. I just felt as if someone was trying to get in touch with me and the connection was lost. I guess an easy way to describe it is like a computer with a dial up server with a computer. For whatever reason, that call disconnected.

Who knows, maybe someday, I will make that connection with that spirit again, and find out who they were, and what they are trying tell me.

## In the Light

John and I were fast asleep in the bedroom. It was around four in the morning. I was awoken from a dead sleep when I heard a strange sound coming from the CD player. I nudged John awake and he asked me, "Why did I put a CD on so damned early in the morning?"

I said, "I didn't!", and I reached to turn the lamp on. Then I jumped out of the bed. I ran across the room to the corner where the stereo was. Everything was off, we had not been listening to it for days at this point. I flipped open the CD player and it was playing Led Zeppelin, *In the Light*.

What kind of joke was this? What message was being given to us on a continuous basis? These experiences were too frequent for us.

Happening more and more often, one after the next. Why?

The next day I was at work, and I normally got out of work at five o'clock each day but for whatever reason I was held back a few minutes at work. John was in the shower, and left the bathroom door open being that nobody else was home. He said as he was showering the shower curtain was pulled open. He looked down, and thought it was me, describing a five foot three woman with reddish brown hair. She looked up at him and walked out of the bathroom. He pulled the curtain closed again, and finished up. By the time he did finish up his shower I really did make it home and walked in the apartment.

As I walked in, he came out of the bathroom with the towel wrapped around him. He asked, "Why did you do that?" I gave him a funny look and said, "WHAT? I just walked in John?" I still had my handbag over my shoulder, and the mail in my hand.

He told me what happened! I said, "Holy Shit! Again?" I asked him, "How did you not know it wasn't me?" He said he just assumed it was me. It was around the time I come home. He had soap on his face and at a quick glance same physical resemblance as me.

Who was this woman now? Was this a form of a future me transcendentally traveling? Or was this a spirit trying to look like me to fool my boyfriend? It was harmless enough but still made us wonder.

Another evening I went out to a diner with my two oldest friend's Beth and Rose, and John stayed home to watch basketball. When I got home, he said he saw a cat. I said, "No shit! We have one!" and I laughed. He was annoyed at me for not taking him more seriously. I realized he was upset so I said, "Ok, Ok, Ok, I am sorry. What happened? " He said, "I was sitting here on the couch watching TV and an all-black cat, well parts of the cat, appeared, then disappeared. First the head, then I saw the mid-section, then the tail end like it was going in and out of dimensions like it was solid, and here and not here. It was the weirdest sight I ever witnessed!"

Eventually Tina and Sandra announced they were selling the apartment building that used to be their childhood home. I guess they had enough of dealing with tenants complaint's, and not up keeping the place as they should of.

And like I always say nothing is ever a coincidence. The man who actually ended up buying that building was a man who used to be friends with John. They were buddies from their youth.

This man, I shall call him 'Bill', asked John to help him do some demo work in the basement.

This is where Beulah used to live. He wanted to renovate it into a nicer apartment to rent it out for higher money. As they were ripping the wall apart and tearing down the old wooden stairwell, an old yellow envelope popped out. It had really old photographs inside. They were real photos of the former politician and deceased owner, Mr. DiBello. These were very provocative nude photos of him with women, several women in the act of sex, and other things. I guess his family never knew these were buried all these years in the walls of their home! I wonder perhaps if Beulah was one of his lovers and that is why they kept her living down there?

Well, let's say Bill, the new owner, kept the pictures and he became greedy and raised the rent every month until we moved out! This was fine by us anyway. He did us a favor.  Too many strange event's kept happening to us there.

## Monks of Sorrow

Less than a year of me moving into my apartment I met my now husband, then boyfriend, at a friend's Halloween party.  Shortly after the New Year, he moved into the apartment with me.  I mentioned to him Beulah, who lived downstairs, would scream about demons and witches and such and that I had also experienced a couple of strange things happen in my apartment.  He shrugged it off. He wasn't a skeptic because he had a few experiences as a child. He had an open mind.  But truthfully, he did not expect to have any experiences either.

One night, he said I slept solidly, right through one of the most terrifying experiences of his life.  He tried to get my attention, and to get me to wake up, but I would not budge. He said that one night while he was still awake just lying there, a man suddenly appeared to him in the room.  The man was in a white monks robe and a roped belt. He had a dark beard and wavy shoulder length hair.

John was frozen with fear, and did not know what to do. He looked over at me and I was out like a light. He tried moving around, causing the bed to bounce and hoping I would awaken to see it, but I never did. The man looked sorrowfully at John, then, shook his head back and forth like he felt bad for him. He said this man was solid and vivid as you and I standing here today. Then, he said the man just vanished. Not a fade away. But he just popped out of this realm of existence, in a "Now he is here, now he isn't," sort of way.

I really wish I could have woken up to see this!  But this experience was not meant for me. Sometimes we get visited for special reasons, and sometimes those reasons we will never know until the time is right in our lives.

# CHAPTER ✎16✎

AUNTY ANNA'S GOODBYE

My Aunty Anna was one of my mothers' sister's. She had a different father than my mom and my Aunt Mame. I was named Ann, (my middle name) after her. She was always full of life and smiling, joking. No matter what, when you looked at her, she was dancing and singing. My two aunts' were like Christmas Day 365 days a year. I loved when they were around or when we visited them. Through the years Aunty Anna's health was declining and Aunt Mame would have concerns about her nutrition and weight. She slowly suffered from dementia and her son, Tom, placed her in a nursing home one Mother's day without telling anyone. He had all legal rights signed over to him. Her home, her bank account, everything. He had a huge tag sale on her front lawn and sold all of her belongings. Then he sold the very home that she and her beloved husband, Jake, built, brick by brick. Tom never did go back and visit his mother. By the time we found out about what he had done, it had been at least a month. We felt helpless. The only thing we could do at this point was visit her, and love her. And we did.

Once late December morning in 2006, I woke up and went into the living room where my then boyfriend, soon to be husband was on the couch. He looked up at me and asked me "What's wrong?" I said, "Aunty is going to pass away very soon. She said goodbye to me in a dream just now." He looked at me like I was out of my mind.

The dream consisted of me in front of an old worn home but with pillars in front of it. There were vines climbing all around the pillars. My two aunts, Mame and Anna, were there. I was walking towards my car in their driveway. I turned to say goodbye to both of them. When I went to kiss Aunt Mame first, my Aunty Anna pulled me away from her and said, "No dear you have to say goodbye to me!" She then grabbed my face with her two hands as she did when I was a child. She kissed me and squeezed me hard.

On January 13<sup>th</sup> 2007, I received the word that she had passed away in her nursing home bed. I was saddened but I expected this. I knew she was once again with her husband, my uncle Jake. She was no longer a prisoner of dementia or that nursing home.

I am happy that I got to say goodbye to her. She was so loving and I will miss her until I see her again.

# CHAPTER ❧17❧

## GRANDDAUGHTER FROM ANOTHER LIFE TIME

My aunt Mame was a wonderful woman. She lived ninety-two years and passed on Sept 16th, 2013. I wanted to share this story, which I know she didn't share with too many people with because of fear of what they may think of her.

She was a woman of great logic and much sense. She was a retired IBM'er. She raised her son alone after the death of her husband Rudy when she was only twenty-eight years old. She never re-married and concentrated on her son and making a home for them. They lived in Pine Plains, New York.

In the 1980's, well after her son moved out and got married, she now lived alone in this cottage that they had made a home for the last forty-plus years. She would wake every morning at four AM and have her coffee, pack her lunch, and proceed to drive to IBM to start her workday. She was well respected and well loved. She wasn't one who lingered in the unknown, or on what seemed to her to be the un-natural.

Many times after work, she would stop by my Aunty Anna's home, about two miles down the road, to see how she was, or if she needed anything. She would then stop at Pecks Market, to pick up last minute dinner ingredients. She had a routine and was used to it. On the weekends, she, and my other aunt would often go to flea markets and second hand shops to pick up different items to refurbish. They were set in their ways.

One day, on a bright and sunny day Saturday afternoon, my aunt Mame was in her living room watching a television program and decided to get up to make tea on the commercial break. As she returned to her living room she noticed a young girl in Victorian clothing on her stairway coming down to her. Her arms were extended and the girl was silent. My aunt said she burst into tears and cried out "Granddaughter!" The girl quickly faded away and Aunt Mame never saw her again.

She explained it to be a rush of emotion; that she knew exactly who the girl was, but did not have her name. She said it happened so quickly, and was over in a blink, but she knew that girl was a part of her, from another lifetime. Her son in this life was an only child and had never had any children after he was married.

I believe our relatives from other lifetimes do come through to us at the moment when we least expect it to happen. She shared this with me timidly but me knowing her as I did, knowing she was never one to dabble in the paranormal or take much stake in it, I know she was sharing a wonderful gift with me. And yes, now, I am sharing it with you.

# CHAPTER ᦥ18ᦥ

## DO YOU TAKE CREAM AND SUGAR?

While my husband I lived in Yonkers, New York, my friend, Rose asked if we wanted to rent the available third floor apartment in her house? We were in need of an apartment at the right price. Her place was one block from the parkway and it was the right price. It was an adorable third floor, walkup, attic apartment. It was a one bedroom; eat in kitchen, living room apartment. The whole story with this apartment has a back drop of course!

Rose had previously rented that apartment to our friend's Beth and Tom. Beth is also best friend to Rose' and myself being that we all grew up with each other. Tom was Beth's husband. They rented that apartment when they were newlyweds. Before Tom and Beth had that apartment, our other friends, Clark and Kate rented that apartment before moving to the second floor, where Clark eventually passed away from cancer in his bed. Clark and Kate were meant for each other. They were so over the moon in love with each other. In their case time and death really does not exist, love goes on.

All of us through the years were great friends. We all used to go out and rent movies, have cookout's in Rose's yard, have New Year's Eve parties—just good times—good people. Then Clark was diagnosed with Prostate cancer and slowly his money ran out and he lost his job. But he never lost his sense of humor or his love for Kate. They became even closer. The night came when his family was surrounding his bed and he took his last breath. His love and beautiful soul will always live on in all of us. His laughter, and his memories. Kate eventually moved out of state.

So, this brings me full circle to my husband and me renting that third floor apartment again. Doesn't it? You thought I went off on some tangent never to return huh? I believe that third floor apartment was where Clark and Kate were at their happiest. It was before the cancer. It was when everyone would pile into that cozy apartment and have a party on any given summer night. It was a special place for many people, for many special people.

So one day after my husband and I were well moved in, I was trying to prepare coffee in the kitchen. I had flipped the switch on the Mr. Coffee machine to get it started when John called me into the living room to look at something on the television. I said, "OK." I finished watching what he showed me and headed back to the kitchen. I was startled at first, but I knew who did it. I found my coffee mug out in front of the Mr. Coffee pot along with the carton of milk and the sugar server with a spoon ready for me. I definitely did not get this far. I smiled and said, "Thank You Clark!" I knew he was still around and helping out. I hope he also poured himself a cup of coffee as well!

# CHAPTER ✎19✎

HOUSE HUNTING...I MEAN HOUSE HAUNTING

It was the fall of 2006, my husband and I were still living in Yonkers, New York. We were thinking of moving upstate to Dutchess County. Each week, John and I would browse through several MLS's and mark off and print out potential homes within our budget. Then I would contact our realtor, and we would meet with him on the following Saturday to see these homes in person.

We were both very excited, as hopeful first time homebuyers would be. One particular Saturday morning, we woke up around six am, in order to be able to make sure we were at the realtor's Hopewell Junction office by eight-thirty.

I needed my coffee badly. As we drove up the winding Taconic Parkway, the father north we drove, the crisp autumn air was slowly turning the leaves. We got off the exit, and onto Route 82 to the Hopewell office. We pulled into the parking lot, and I turned off the car. We did not immediately see our realtor's car. The office was still closed.

We waited in the car, occasionally checking the car radio clock, ten minutes, fifteen minutes, twenty minutes; finally, we see a woman approach the office, and let herself in with a key. We figure, well our realtor, Jake can't be far behind.

Thirty-minutes have passed—no sign of Jake, our realtor. I was pissed because I make it a point of being early to appointments. We got out of the car and walked into the realtor's office. The woman behind the desk smiled and asked "May I help you?" I said, "Well, you can start with finding our very late realtor, Jake." She said, "Oh I saw you sitting outside in your car this whole time. I had no idea you were waiting for him." She took her cell phone and slipped into an empty office and shut the door behind herself.

I heard mumbled talking. Unable to make out exact words. She came out, smiled, and said, "Please have a seat. Can I get you coffee?

Jake should be here in thirty minutes, he lost power at his home and he overslept. He is so sorry."

John and I were annoyed, but we traveled this far and felt what is a little longer going to hurt. We sat in the reception area drinking terrible instant coffee and flipping through last year's magazines.

Just about thirty-five minutes later Jake's PT Cruiser pulls into the lot at a feverish speed and he parked crooked. He hops out in a hurry and runs in apologizing all over himself. He grabs some stale coffee in his thermos and picks up some last minute papers. He ushers us to his car and we pile into his car. He looks hung over and tells us he has a head cold and overslept due to Nyquil, not realizing his co-worker told us that he had a power outage. We dismiss it, and want to get the day started already.

One of the homes I had picked out to look out was in Stanfordville NY, off Route 82. It was across from the old Chapel and was on two acres of land. As we pulled up to it you an tell the pictures were photoshopped, because in person this house cried out for help. It was in definite need of a face-lift. This thing was sorrowful. It was perhaps too much for our tight budget to handle. But we were there and no sense in NOT looking at this point.

As the realtor opened the door with his key, what we noticed next was one of the most unusual things I have seen in my life. I think it would be fair to say in any one of our three lives. It was way past the peculiar, and downright whacko!

The front door opened up to the living room. In the living room there was a rocking chair set up

with a huge ceramic bust of Jesus Christ facing the door. To say the least, it was unsettling to see. The realtor cleared his throat in a nervous fashion and looked at the two of us. I guess feeling us out for a reaction. John and I looked at each other and raised our eyebrows and shrugged it off like "What in the world? " But we entered the living room, and as we stood in the living room speaking to each other, we then heard a loud bang upstairs, a door slamming. Jake, our realtor called out "Hello?" He said, "Oh perhaps there is another realtor here showing it." But we did not see any other cars outside so how that could even are possible? No one answered us.

My eyes kept focusing on Jesus in the rocking chair. I just knew there was a country song waiting to be written here someplace. My mind wandered to picturing Willie Nelson's next big hit being, "Jesus in a Rocking Chair." The lyrics would go something like this "Oh lord let my problems disappear as I rock in this chair." Now I knew I was bored! Writing country songs for Willie Nelson in my head!

At that moment, all three of us heard footsteps on the second floor. Then they stopped. "Hello," we all called out." "Maybe squatters," I said. "Or maybe it's haunted?" At that, Jake, the realtor, said, "I am going back out to the car. The two of you can look through the house if you wish. Let me know your thoughts of the home."

John took off for the second floor as I wandered around the rest of the first floor. I walked into the bathroom, which was handicap accessible, extra wide doorway, handles on the shower walls, and an extra wide toilet bowl with an enforced seat and bar grips. I noticed a door across from the toilet bowl. I assumed it was a linen closet. When I opened the door it was a long narrowed set of stairs leading to the attic. I began going up the steps. The odor was musty, and the stream of dust particles was visible through a crack of light coming from a poorly insulated roof shingle. To my left there was a box of naked dolls, with blinking eyes. Some of the eyes were open and some were stuck. Some of the dolls were missing limbs. At that point I didn't know what was creepier, the Jesus in the rocking chair, or the friggin' dolls.

I heard John calling for me so I backed down the creaky attic steps and I shut the bathroom door behind me, meeting John back in the living room. He said the upstairs had so many leaky ceiling tiles that chances the whole roof had to be redone. We shook our heads NO, NO, NO, and HELLS NO. We had enough.

Just then, the screen door opened and slammed shut. We thought Jake came back into the house. We called out, "Jake? Hello?" No Jake. So we left the house and went back to Jake's car. Jake got out and locked up the house. There was a definite negative vibe there in that place.

Jake came back into the car and asked us how we liked it. We said we didn't. Too much work to be done for too much money. Then I asked Jake if he believed in ghosts, and I caught his look through the rear view mirror at me. He did not look amused at all. In fact he looked terrified. He said, "Well, there were some strange things that I can't explain that happened in there. I can tell you that. I hope no one else wants to look at that house with me."

So is it haunted? Who knows but I can tell you that there were strange occurrences that went on there that afternoon.

# CHAPTER ❧20❧

## MY SAMHAIN BLESSING 2012

Samhain is a time to honor your deceased loved ones, and bring in the New Year for pagans. The veil between the living and the dead become one, and the dead walk amongst the living. As I prepare my home for the holiday, I often think about my loved ones that have gone on before me. I light white candles and I pray for them with love. This particular Samhain they decided to pay me a little visit and so now let me go on to tell you how they showed their calling card to me tongue in ghost cheek!

This year I had recently lost my dear Aunt Mame, on Sept 16th. I didn't find out until ten days later when she had been long buried. My sister and I had not even had known she was ill in the hospital, dying. Our cousin, her son, Mike never called us. It took my sister sending a 'thinking of you' card to my aunt's home that was read by my cousins' wife for us to find out. His wife called and dropped that bomb on us. The call came out of nowhere and was lacking in any kind of emotion or respect. She said, "Oh, it's Carol, your aunt died ten days ago." Our beloved Mame—gone. I felt cheated out of seeing her one last time. I felt I had no closure. I felt angry at my cousin for not calling us.

On October 31st, 2013 my husband and I decided to drive over to the grave site with a mini pumpkin to place on her grave and to pay my respects. We drove up through the gate of the cemetery and the skies were charcoal gray as black crows circled in the winds above cawing as if they were announcing my arrival to some unseen forces that I had not been made aware of.

I spotted a care taker shoveling, so we parked, and walked up to him. He introduced himself as Allen, and I inquired about where my aunt's burial plot was. He nodded and knew right away who I was speaking of. He said, "Yes, Mary! Nice gal. How come you didn't show up?" I explained what had happened then he said he was sorry for my loss.

He proceeded to tell us where the marker was because as of yet, there was not a head stone. We walked over to her marker, I left the mini pumpkin, and I said a little prayer for her. I will miss her always. I am sorry I never got a chance to say goodbye and tell her that I loved her. Although I am sure she knows that I loved her.

We used to talk on the phone for hours. I felt so broken up and weird that it wasn't real to me that I would never see her again. I always saw her for Halloween. She always made Halloween goody bags, and homemade ceramic Jack-O-Lanterns to place a candle inside for me. She sent me my first kitchen witch to hang in my kitchen. She knew what this holiday meant to me. Halloween/ Samhain would never be the same without Mame.

Besides the fact that it was really cold out that day, I felt numb inside. Winter was setting in. We got back into the car and drove back home. The rest of that say was solemn.

November 1st, I always take all the decorations down and get into the Yule swing mode. So, with that being said, that is how I discovered I had a visit.

When decorating, I had placed three resin skulls lined up on my mantle, with candles in the dining room, along with the autumn dried leaves on a vine, and my ceramic pumpkin votive. I noticed only two skulls on the mantle. I figured as I chuckled to myself, "Uh oh, one of my cats got to it and I will find later in the spring the following year. Then as I pulled apart the mantle, the votive, and so on I noticed that one pumpkin votive was pretty heavy and its opening was facing the wall. The missing resin skull was inside the pumpkin. That would be impossible for any cat to maneuver. The cat could not pull back the ceramic pumpkin votive away from the wall; place the resin skull inside, then, place the pumpkin back neatly against the wall. There would have been broken ceramic everywhere.

I believe that was my aunt's way of acknowledging my visit to her grave and letting me know she was still with me on my special day. That meant the world to me. Magic Happens! Be Blessed.

# CHAPTER ॐ21ॐ

## UNEXPECTED FAMILY REUNION

It was June of 2013, when I was asked to be a production assistant and have a small part in an independent film. I had no idea that it would to leave me with residual after affects.

I was given the chance to portray a real character, her name was Claire. She lived at the Shanley Hotel, located in Napanoch, New York until her untimely passing, in 1905. Her life was a mystery really, no one really knew if she was a call girl, a boarding resident, but she was pregnant with child when she died. They found her hanging in her bedroom on the third floor of the Shanley Hotel. She had been seeing a gentleman caller as well. Rumor is either he left her, or she took her own life, or he had found out she was with child and did not want a scandal so he had her murdered. Until this day many investigators visit that hotel trying to uncover the mystery of Claire.

It really filled me with so much emotion as I read about her and prepared to portray her. I wanted to make sure that I came across in the most respectful way as possibly could. Because of playing Claire, I was lead to meet a very special woman by the name of Virginia Centrillo , and in turn was able to communicate with my deceased loved ones once again. So if it hadn't been for taking this opportunity, I would have never met Virginia, and through Virginia make a wonderful friend as well.

So allow me to describe the day I met Virginia Centrillo.

On the first day of the shoot I was production assistant. We were filming at Miss Fanny's Victorian Party House, located in Wappingers Falls, New York so there was no acting needed on my behalf. My duties were to meet and greet the day's actors, and get them settled, and ready for their filming.

It was summer time and the heat was relentless. As cars pulled up, I basically lead each actor into the Victorian home, got them settled in until they were ready for make-up, and filming their scenes. A car pulled up again, as I walked up to greet the next actor / visitor to the set, a woman got out of the car and she immediately looked up at the bedroom windows. I looked up to see what she was looking at. She was squinting to see, trying to get a really good look. She said very assuredly as she looked at me, "He is up there." I smiled and said, "Ok, let's get you inside and set up.

I went through the instructions I was asked to go through with everyone. I said "We have to shut cell phones off and speak with a whisper." I lead her slowly up the ornately decorated stairs. She turned to me and grabbed her throat, as she looked very startled. Her eyes got big and she said, "Oh No!"

I said, "What is wrong?"

She said she was envisioning someone getting hung. I quickly realized she was psychically gifted. I chuckled, and replied, "Oh you're probably seeing tomorrow. I am acting tomorrow and in my scene is I am being hung." I quickly set her mind as ease.

She chuckled, and said, "Wow you seem too nice to hang though." We both started to giggle.

We settled into the guest room where they set up a green room for the films guest's. She started reading me and said you have many dead family members here. I was caught off guard, but in a pleasant way.

She said, "Who is the strong "A" name that you are named after?"

I said, "My Auntie Anna; Ann being my middle name." She then went onto to say she was with you when you had a recent car accident. I started to tear up. Virginia could have never known any of this. This was something you could not have Googled about me.

She went on to say, "Who is the strong "G" name? He is saying something about electricity? He states he is good at math now." I started to laugh. It was my dad. It was his way of showing me it really was him. He absolutely sucked at math while on earth. I take after him in that nature. And the electric, well, as we were growing up he would go through the house shutting the lights off saying "Jezuz Christ shut deese lights off. I'm not fuckin' Con Ed!" And now that is drilled into my head now too! My dad was really watching out for me. She also said that my father in law came in for a moment; he had died earlier that year. She said a man is stepping forward to say he had a leg injury, then, he had a brain injury, and died. Well, my father in law had a bad leg, had a stroke eventually, brain cancer, and then he passed.

As we sat in that room, Virginia said my children were coming through.

I said, "I don't have any children."

She smiled and said, "Yes you did. You lost pregnancies, two of them, and they are recognizing their dad, a fire fighter." I almost passed out.

I said, "That was a lifetime ago."

She said, "They are there and that was their way of validating themselves to you."

Then, Virginia's attention went to the other side of the room and said there was a woman with blonde hair pointing at a box. No name was coming up and she wanted us to know she was there. I said, "Well, this is my friend Julie's bedroom, maybe she has information about the box." When Julie came back Virginia asked Julie about who the blonde woman was and what could be in that box. Julie explained the friend with blonde hair was her deceased friend, and the box contained her friends' ashes. So that validated that without any other questions.

So it's not every person that states they have this gift of psychic ability I believe, but when you spend an afternoon such as the one I spent with Virginia out of the blue, I must say Virginia is solid gold and pure love. I can't thank her enough for that day! It was so unexpected. That day and those messages will never leave me.

Thank you Virginia, I love you!

If you are interested in contacting Virgina Centrillo please visit www.theppa.net.

Donna Parish-Bischoff

# CHAPTER ᕙ22ᕗ

MERRY CHRISTMAS, WITH LOVE, FROM HEAVEN

I felt the need to share this wonderful experience I had today. It doesn't fall into the field of the paranormal and certainly doesn't strike me as a frightening moment. If you're looking for a spine tingling tale or looking to find an uplifting, heart-warming faith in knowing our loved ones still watch over us, even long after they are physically gone off the planet— keep reading.

Date of happening: December 22$^{nd}$, 2012 approximate time 11:30 a.m.

Location: CVS Pharmacy, Poughkeepsie, NY, Photo Kiosk Dept.

I was with my husband, and I had a ton of family photos to scan for my sister to make a small family album for her as part of her Christmas gift. My husband was walking around the store to kill time and occasionally checked on me from time to time.

This past year my health has not been the greatest, and I woke up that morning feeling achy, with a migraine; it is part of my condition I am suffering from. I had also been going through my usual Holiday blues of missing my family members that are no longer with us. Feeling sad remembering the great holidays as a kid with all of them. I guess you can say a touch of self-pity was seeping in.

As each photo was being scanned, I would remove them from the scanner and place them into the folder I brought them in. As I lifted the scanner top, I noticed there was a note in my grandmothers' hand writing on the back of a photo of her from when she first came to this country. Originally, I was in such a rush I hadn't taken notice. As I lifted the picture up to read what it said, I suddenly felt a chill go up my spine and felt my hair stand on edge.

It read *Dear Donna I hope you feel better. I love you, Grandma.*

My grandmother wrote a note at least thirty-five or forty years ago to me!

My eye's welled up with water at that moment, and I just had this feeling come over me of pure love! That she was reaching out to me in some way. Making sure I saw that old note that resonated the message she needed to deliver to me that moment.

It sure did feel good to read it again after all these years.

I love you too Grandma!  Merry Christmas in Heaven

# CHAPTER ❧23❧

## DONNA PARISH-BISCHOFF, PARANORMAL INVESTIGATOR

When I tell people that I am a paranormal investigator, I get two reactions. One reaction is the double take and dramatic roll of the eyes. At that moment, if, I had any chance, to receive respect from this individual, all hopes are now shot down the proverbial toilet! The other reaction is that persons' pupils grow larger, they draw closer almost as though they are a little kid on Halloween waiting to hear a juicy ghost story followed by I love that "stuff," Stuff? Stuff? Stuff being dead people? Spirits? Ghosts?

It is a broad spectrum. People do not realize this. They gush, "Oh that is so cool," followed by their personal haunted tales. I prefer the latter of the reactions, but we can't always get what we want.

We often cling to our faith and spiritual beliefs, and lack of those as well. I get many non-believers come up to me and try to challenge me. I am not one to be challenged. I will just walk away. Why? Well because I believe in what I believe in and I respect what they believe in.

To each his own. I am not here to force my beliefs onto others. I am not here to make anyone believe in the afterlife. That is a personal choice. But, if someone asks me what I think, I tell him or her.

Overall, it comforts us to know there is a greater power watching over us.

Different spiritual beliefs bring on many, different feelings. I have seen people so overcome by emotion on investigations where there are tears streaming down their face. Our bodies react differently as well while on investigations. The best piece of Paranormal equipment you have is YOU!

We pick up on feeling's that vibrate from the past. If we touch an object, we may begin

to see images, feel emotions that are not of our own. This is called psychometry. Psychometry is a psychic ability in which a person can sense or "read" the history of an object by touching it. Such a person can receive impressions from an object by holding it in his/her hands, or perhaps, touching it to the forehead. Such impressions may be perceived as images, sounds, smells, tastes – even emotions.

In other words, using your 'gut instinct,' and slapping a fancy title to it. I believe that we all have the ability to pick up on impressions. This doesn't make us "Psychic." We have these antenna's you could say, or the hair on the back of your neck stands up, you get a chill, etc. I always say, "Go with your gut."

There was one woman that I met in an adult education class back in the late 1980's. We were given a task to try, after we completed this particular phase of the lesson. We handed each other our key rings and we sat with a pen and paper, holding the objects.

Collecting data mentally is a neat little exercise to help you hone in on your natural God or Goddess given gifts. I began to get a picture of a college aged male. He was wearing glasses. With a poor complexion, acne scarred, oily, and pale. I kept getting the word deficiency in my mind. She said the image I got was that of her son, who fit the description I gave, and that he had been seeing a doctor for B-12 shots.

So I amazed myself at how easy it is to open yourself to using your own mind to be a Tool. In the paranormal field I have come to find (for myself, for the moment anyway), that I tend to gravitate to the calmer way of performing the investigations. I do not find that provocation is my answer to getting reactions. I find it stirs the pot. The question is, What is in that pot? Then, (after you and your team pack up and leave) think of the poor client that now has to live with that mess you have caused.

Picture this if you will:  You and your family are sitting around the TV watching a movie or a show. All of a sudden total strangers barge in your home, uninvited, rude, and demanding. They start yelling at you, using profanity. That would make you terribly upset. Wouldn't it?

Well that is what we do every time we do a Paranormal Investigation. You are stepping into their environment. You are the guest here. Be a polite houseguest if you want them to communicate with you.

We often get audio of an EVP (Electronic Voice Phenomenon) simply stating that traditional phrase many investigators get on audio, "GET OUT!"

I will often take the approach, somewhat the same way I would when meeting a person for the first time, and I introduce myself when I open up an EVP Session. I say, *Hello, I am Donna. I am here in respect of your lovely home. Thank you for having us.* Then, if I have any prior history on the home or location, or if I have history of who the client thinks it may be, I will let the spirit understand that our equipment placed around will never hurt them if they choose to walk near us. I ask them if we can help them with anything at all. I ask if there is anything, they need or want. Perhaps a message passed onto to someone that is still living. I make them understand I am not there to cause further anguish or pain, but the opposite, I would like to help them move on if they choose to do so.

I find if you are respectful and kind, they may be willing to answer your questions or tell you more about who they are. More flies with honey so to speak.

When I am done with the EVP Session, I close it out by saying *Thank you again for allowing me into your lovely home. I appreciate it.* Then I say goodbye.

Now there are people out there who really do not know how we get these EVP's. I use a digital recorder they can range anywhere from $30.00 to $200.00. I personally use a cheaper one I paid under $40.00 in an electronic store. Major bulk stores even carry them. They run for hours so they are terrific. They come with a USB cord to hook directly into your computer. They also have a CD to upload the program nationally. Then as you listen to them, when you come across something you believe could be an EVP, you simply crop the sound byte. I normally listen to it several times, over and over, to determine factors. Process of elimination. You can save it as an MP3 on your computer.

I often get asked the question, *Do you really believe in ghosts?* Well my answer is always quite simple, yes. Why else would a forty-five year old, married woman, with a full time job spend most weekend nights in someone's dark, spider infested, and dusty basement speaking into the air and holding a K-2 meter? The answer is always, yes, I believe.

The other question I am often asked is, *Why do I do what I do?* Well that answer is not so quite simply stated. There are various reasons why one does this. For me there are a combination of reasons. Because I want to research what used to scare the hell out of me as a child growing up on Lee Avenue. If anyone read my first book, you will get it right away. Because I know that, there is an existence to what happens after our hearts stop beating. I do it in case there is a wandering spirit who needs to move forward, but perhaps could be stuck, scared, confused as far as what happened to them. Because I believe that earth and the heavens are possibly separated by a thin invisible layer, which at the right moment coincide with one another causing tiny little Vortexes.

They can walk freely into our world, but we cannot go into theirs whenever we want, while wide-awake and conscious. This intrigues me because I know through learning about this that you can try T.M.

(Transcendental Meditation), or you can sometimes float in a dream state, but maybe because we are weighed down by our bodily existence that keeps us from entering their world. Who really knows? Right?

Well that is why I would like to pry into much of it to get a looky-see. Many investigations they are not resolved inside of thirty minutes or less like a television show. We do our best to dig as much history as possible, locations, dates, and people who have lived or worked at a location. If the location was re-located as many buildings were back in the day, your best bet is to Google the location, go to City Hall, and pay a buck for photocopies of blue print's or information, which is all public domain.

We sit with the clients, interview them, and see who else in their home has had an experience to share. We often keep in touch with the client because sometimes we re-visit the site, hand over copies of whatever evidence we have captured. We want the client to feel at ease and trust us as a friend. We have even had clients been so well versed in the investigating, that they became investigators themselves. It's good to take the fear out of it. It makes me feel as if I approached the situation in the correct respect that it deserved.

Now with that being said, there is a whole new and different side to "some" client's. Some people call an investigator and have claims that curl even my hair! I again have to take it seriously and at face value until we actually get out to the location and assess what needs to be done. The thing that gets me is the client that has us into their homes and makes no attempt to tidy up or put away any items that maybe considered 'personal'. Use your imagination's here.

They also watch these crazy television shows and insist that Satan used to own their home and still visits. Some people (not many) BUT some past clients I have come to the conclusion that they either want attention or have a substance abuse issue. That is not my area of expertise. So we file those investigations as unfounded and not haunted.

I am not saying that because you do not have a clean house your house isn't haunted. But if you do not take steps to listen, or take advice, and seemingly keep inviting the entity back, then we cannot help you. The homeowners must be strong and be a part of the solution to rid their home of the negativity. If we come in and do a house blessing, or sage burning with prayers. Then we leave and the client starts to speak to it again, you are confusing the spirit. It does not know if it should leave or stay. IGNORE it after the blessing. Stop looking for it to pop up around the corners. Be assertive.

Take your home back. It is no longer their home. You pay the mortgage or rent. The spirit does not. Be respectful but be firm.

Be careful what you wish for. So many paranormal investigators and groups, and there are *thousands* of them out there, try to get a name for themselves on TV. Everyone is a reality TV star these days. Some of the shows are really good and some, just really bad. The ones to look for must be respectful of the homeowners, of the investigators, and they are accommodating. The bad ones ask you to lie and stir things up to create ratings. Those are the ones to walk away from. More than likely, they will make you sign on the dotted line. You will be told you are owed minimal money when you should be getting way more, BUT don't know any better. They smile in your face, so you think it's all good and they are friendly, so they must be telling you the truth. Read your contract twice and thrice over with a magnifying glass. All your hard-earned investigative theories and footage will not belong to you.

Kiss it goodbye. Once you sign, YOU cannot back out otherwise you will be sued. You will think a person is your friend and they will smile, BUT business is business. So believe me when I tell you it's great to want to get your team on TV and get your word out there. To want to help people. But it's quite another to be told to act scared on screen when you know you're NOT. I am not saying don't apply for TV shows. I am just saying do your homework, and realize it's not all roses and sunshine. And if you are ok with that, then go for it, but remember that there is re-run hell, and you will get e-mails asking why you sold out from the Para community, Social Network comments, and a slew of other backlash. And if you sell out, IT will show in the work that you do. So, do all of your homework before you decide 100% that you want to be on a Paranormal show. Perhaps make a DVD of your team, compile a few investigations with evidence, and submit it to your local cable company for local access for free.

I would try that first. You won't sell out and you will stay true to yourself.

## The Physical Part about Being a Paranormal Investigator

More than likely if you're a paranormal investigator that has been doing it a while you will come to agree with me that it takes its toll on your body. At time, your physical well being as well as your emotional outlook. It's addictive and draining at the same time. It's that double edged sword. Sure it's an adrenaline rush but sometimes at what cost?

To those who do not investigate the paranormal or as the non-believer's call it, as they giggle like little girls with pictures of that 1980's movie mocking the whole process, "ghost busters."

It really is serious business to those who take it on, face to face and heart to heart to help those in genuine need. I can tell you from my own stand point view that our team takes precautions before and after an investigation. Trust me you never know if you're dealing with a spirit that is positive or negative or a spirit at all. We come from diverse faith backgrounds, but the one thing that remains intact is that we are all for the good. We bless ourselves, say prayers during the investigation, and ask the presence not to follow us home. BUT that doesn't always guarantee it won't thumb a ride with you to the next town. You may begin to suddenly feel depressed after an investigation, but you felt absolutely cheerful prior, and have no history of depression. You may absorb the feelings you are picking up from the entity, and are acting as a "conductor" or an "empath," an extension cord for their feelings to come out of, if you will. You may begin to feel ill physically, nausea, dizzy. This is all residual spirit energy.

Remember Paranormal Investigating is not a board game you can fold up and throw up on the closet shelf at the end of the night. You have the responsibility here since you opened the door of communication. This is why I do not recommend "back to back" investigations, weekend after weekend. Sure it's cool to be wanted to ask for, BUT you need time to recuperate, heal, go over evidence, and discuss the investigation with your team mates.

When you start these back to back investigations, you will begin to notice you will always be coming down with a cold, a flu bug, an ailment, etc. Trust me at least on this much. You cannot help another spirit if your own spirit needs re-charging.

This year alone I have experienced several illnesses and accidents. So I am taking my own advice, slowing down, and spacing my investigations apart. Quality is far better than quantity. You need to give your best, not you're all.

## Why Do Ghosts Suddenly Appear When You Are Near?

Why do some spirits remain wandering the earth? Is it like a time stamp? A footprint left behind? A passage of time that replays itself over and over like a looped tape? That would be considered a *residual haunting* to a paranormal investigator. An *intelligent haunting* seems to communicate or respond accordingly with what you do or say to them. They can happen at any time of day, or any room of the location in question.

If you feel willing enough, these would be theories to test out.

Are these intelligent hauntings? Or residual ones that just play over and over and have no interaction at all with what goes on around them.

Do we bring spirits with us? Are we like sponges? Some of us are. Some of us are not.

Maybe it's just as plain and simple as a spirit that has connection to a particular person for a reason. It could be a familiarity that the spirit has with the person. For whatever reason, that spirit reached out to that person for help, or to get a message across. It is up to us to follow through with this mission.

So many people get locked up inside and fear it, or start to scream at the spirit thinking it's evil right off the bat. To begin with, all it is trying to do is get your attention and mustering up enough energy to so, is exhausting. So obviously anything it ends up doing successfully will be done clumsily and misunderstood. Ending in mass hysteria on your part. You do not need to call in the big guns at first right away that is. You are completely capable of communicating with these spirits yourself at first. Using a respectful tone. That is. Always be respectful. That is the key here.

So many people ask me, *Why are things getting worse?* I turn it around and ask them, *Tell me what you did?*

They begin with, "Well I screamed, 'Get the fuck outta my house, you mother fucka!' Then I got my Ouija Board out and performed a one person Séance."

I think, to myself, *um, you did WHAT? Oh boy, yes well now you have opened up a can of worms, and created a shit storm for yourself my friend.* Doing something like this is like smothering yourself in honey and standing in front of a bears' den on the first day of spring. It's not recommended, EVER! Please refrain from that.

Ask it some simple, polite questions, and record yourself while asking the questions. Ask them if they have a message you can get to someone for them. Is there something that they need? You may also want to use sage to bless your home. This is also known as *smudging*. When you do this, you should open the windows in your home so that the negative will is released with the smoke.

There is no wrong way to bless your home you can recite any words that make you feel at peace.

I have some words below as an example:

Say these words, *May the white light and divine love and protection surround me.* Keep saying these words as you go from room to room. Go from the top of every door way and window, from every corner of the room outward until you walk to the exit of the home.

When you are done, very simply and kindly say, *I ask that any negative energy please vacate my home in the name of white light and all that is good. I mean you no harm and want to help you.*

## Skepticism

We question everything. As we should. It's in the fibers of our souls to do so. It's good to do so. Question everything until you can't do it any longer. We are taught the laws of science from the ripe age of zero. Since before we leave our mothers' womb. We have gadgets being hooked up to our mother's bellies to document our movements, snap our pictures before we grow ears and noses, and play Mozart for us to brain wash us to be a genius popping performing a Sonata in an instant!

Weighing the probabilities of science and man, things that happen right in front of us and things that we say that happened right in front of us. Then we ask did anyone else see it? Were there cameras rolling? Ah… Our buddy skepticism comes strolling in.

One person's word against another. If it didn't happen on video or in front of two people then it was nothing more than a personal experience. Then we cast it away as nothing?

Oh boy! How rotten is that for that person who had this Holy Grail of a paranormal moment?

Sadly, when on a paranormal investigation at a location we have to work it that way when handing over evidence to clients because they can't go by what just one investigator saw or felt while being alone in one room with no equipment running. It can cause our team to look as if we are falsifying our evidence. So we have no choice but to professionally throw it out the proverbial window for our own sake.

When we are at a location and it is in full throttle, we set up teams of 2 to 3 people in each part of the location. They all are armed with recorders, cameras, running video, and most importantly eyeballs. They can all vouch for each other, and when something happens they collectively see it, feel it, hear it, etc., and we can share that with confidence with a client. That eliminates the skepticism right away.

Then we also have those who have come along on our teams that come to see an entity, and have NEVER, EVER seen anything paranormal in their life, and they want to ride that wave to see what the fuss is about. In the end, I go through hours of audio of hearing them complain how cold they are, how tired they are, how hungry they, how they haven't see a ghost yet, how far from home they are, and they want to see a ghost. Oh My God! I have had to eliminate asking them back, not because they don't believe but because they don't shut up long enough for a Spirit to want to show up.

The poor spirit is probably thinking what a bunch of whiney ghost hunters and flew back up to the attic to sleep! So if you don't believe that is fine but you must be patient. It may never happen for you, OR it may happen in its own time for you. Don't ruin it for other groups doing their work. There are clients at stake as well.

## Brain Function and The After life

I have been watching these documentaries and reading articles on brain function and the afterlife. So many scientists and doctors claim that it is nothing more than a hallucination. They say that our brains release endorphins and dopamine to help with the process of dying to make it a more pleasant experience. They flat out refuse to believe in the real possibility that the afterlife actually does exist.

So many people have given reports of real experiences. These people describe the same visions over and over. How do the same people who have never met describe the same place? Visually? Please tell me someone? Indulge me! I really want to know.

What I do believe is that our bodies do provide a natural pain killer, I do not deny that. However I do not feel these natural pain killers provide us with the ability to float outside our bodies and see above the rooms we are in, and float into other rooms and see our loved ones going about their daily routines, or see our loved ones on the other side waiting for us.

I placed a request for people to reach out to me regarding this subject. I asked them to share their stories of near death experiences. I believe the responses I received to be accurate and sincere. I received hundreds of responses and although I would love to post each of the responses, I have chosen a few as examples to share. I am also sharing my own experience with all of you.

Many years ago I had surgery at Lennox Hill Hospital in Manhattan. My sister, Doreen had driven me down to the city, and waited. It was outpatient surgery. As they wheeled me into the operating room, they asked her to go get some coffee, and they would get her when I was in the recovery room. I remember climbing onto the operating table and seeing the tools they were to use. The nurse told me not to look because I would get frightened. I remember feeling very cold. My butt was hanging out of the thin cotton gown they gave me. I lied down, and they strapped each arm down so I could not move, in case I awoke in the middle of surgery. The nurse took a blanket out of the warmer and covered me. Her name was Siobhan; she had an Irish brogue and calming smile.

My surgeon came in and I remember he looked like K.C. from K.C. and the Sunshine Band. I had to laugh. It was pretty funny. Then the anesthesiologist approached and asked me to count backwards from ten. Well I did not get to nine before I did not remember anything else.

Now flash backward to my sister: She got herself a cup of coffee and moseyed into the gift shop to kill time. She had spotted these adorable plush, stuffed animal piglets. She knew I would love one, but the price was insane and about the same as what it was costing to park that day in a garage. So regretfully she did not purchase it for me. She went back to the waiting area when the nurse called her into the recovery room for me and said I should be waking up any moment. About fifteen minutes later, I was groggy and very out of it, and slowly focusing in on my sister's face. She smiled at me and said how do you feel?

I replied in a raspy, drunken sounding voice, "He was cute." She looked puzzled at me.

She said, "He was cute? Who Donna? The doctor? The nurse?

I shook my head and said, "No, that pig you looked at." If my sister could have fell off her chair at that moment, she would have!

How could I know this? How did I know she was in the gift shop looking at a stuffed pig for me? It was only the two of us. No nurse or doctor left the operating room to spy on her and report and report back to me and whisper in my unconscious ear. I believe I took a little trip that afternoon.

Why? I do not know. Did I flat line and they never told me? Who knows? Was it a form of transcendental meditation? Maybe. The mystery is in the beauty of it. But I recalled the cute, stuffed piglet she was looking at in that gift shop that afternoon while I was under the knife. So many questions with one answer no one seemed to have.

Some added notes about how our brain hemispheres work:

The Right Hemisphere of our brain is associated with creativity and more susceptible of seeing the paranormal entities. It's in our sleeping hours that our meditation, our "Right" sides strengthen. Allowing us to use more of it.

The Left Hemisphere of our brain is associated with skepticism, this tends to be more dominant, analytical, and we are trained by society to go more with the left side. So we let the "Gifts of our Right" side weaken.

For Those Who Do Not Believe No Answer Will Suffice, For Those Who Do Believe No Answer is Necessary

People believe in many things. Different gods' goddesses', angel's demons, Santa Claus, the Easter Bunny, the Tooth Fairy, the Loch Ness Monster, Big Foot, Churro Capra, the monster under your bed the list is endless. Everyone has a lucky number. People will tell they believe in thing's they have never physically seen. It's a deep belief within them, they know, and feel it in their spirit. You have never seen God or Goddess, but you know and feel their presence of existence. It's in the vibration of the Earth. There is proof in everything you touch, see, hear, feel, taste, and what you are. It is the reason why you exist.

There are many people out there that I know personally, that I have investigated cases with, that have never seen or had a paranormal experience in their life, and  yet they go on investigating in hopes to have that one experience that will change their life forever in how they look at the ever after. So far, they still have not had an experience, they are so skeptical and closed to any possibilities, and they seem to have an answer for everything that occurs on every investigation. I appreciate their efforts to debunk and sort out the science from the paranormal. But sometimes you have to say, *What the fuck was that?,* or *Dude I don't have a reasonable theory for that.*

Instead, they say, *Everything has an explanation.*   Really? Everything?  I don't doubt things until I can disprove them; however, the problem is if I can't disprove something then what am I left with?

I encourage all of you to try and debunk before you go around saying this is haunted or that is haunted.  Try and make sense of the senseless first.  Then when you have nothing else–make a decision to believe or not to believe.

People often have a haunting, and at first, they deny it. Why? Because if they pretend it's not there, it's not really happening. They are afraid of it. They don't want to kick up the dust and create more energy, get it riled up, and cause more activity. I can understand and appreciate that. That is why it depends on how you go about your investigation.

As I mentioned earlier, as long as it's with utmost respect and love you should have no problems. If you do it with anger and demands, and you will open up a can of whoop ass on yourself. Do not be afraid to see what is going on in your place whether it is in your shop or home. Set up video cameras at two angles and leave them running. Walk away for the day or night. Leave an audio recorder running, before you leave the recorder

State the date and time, announce who you are, and ask the spirit to speak into the recorder. You will be back later to check the recording, listen to it, and verify if they spoke to you.

Maybe you can answer a question they have for you. It really doesn't have to be a scary thing. You can make it a science project, sort of speaking with someone that lives in another vortex of time. If you look at it in that nature, you may be less nervous. It may take that *ghost hunter* stigma out of the mix for you.

## To Go To the Light or Not To Go To the Light

We often get asked why aren't you always able to make spirits go to the light or send them away? As an investigator, it's our job to inquire as much about the client as possible. We inquire as much as we can about the ground that the house or building it stands on.

Don't get me wrong, we don't ask terribly personal questions, but we need to know if they had a personal connection to the deceased. We may ask some questions, such as how they died, an illness, how old, so on, but Sometimes we do come across that rare occasion where some clients enjoy the attention of holding onto their ghost.

We tell them we have just done a full on investigation and house cleansing, and we also walk the client through what to do in case they would like to follow through and perform their own house blessing after we are gone from the home. But days later we get an e-mail or call back stating, "Nope, nothing worked!" When we ask what happened we find out that against our advice, as soon as we left, the client went around the house shouting, "Are you still here? Hey! Evil demon! Come on out! Are you still here?" When they egg on, or call back these spirits, rather than ignore them and let them go, they invite them back. They are literally anchoring them back.

So spirits go through what I call a *clash* moment. They are undecided, *Should I stay? Or, should I go?* People, you need to be firm and take your home back! If a paranormal group just went through great trouble of taking hours of investigating and doing a cleansing and blessing, then please do your part and leave it be! You cannot acknowledge them once you have done a cleansing. I also suggest you leave out any threats to them or cursing at them when you first discover your entity and have your house blessing. Use respect when speaking with them at all times. I know so many people who enjoy provoking and cursing them, and then wonder why they become ill or have so many problems. They ask themselves, "Why does so much bad luck follow me?" Hmm? Coincidence, I think not?

So heed the advice. When dealing with spirits, it is best to use kindness. It may take some time, but have patience my friends. There may be unfinished business that could be a reason why this spirit cannot move on either. So there may be many reasons why it isn't quite ready, but remember, be kind when dealing with the spirits. You certainly would not want someone bursting into your living room shouting foul things into your face, would you? Well they feel like that is what is happening to them.

They were once living people. At best, they are misunderstood. Take a step back and try to have a heart before jumping.

Hopefully one day we will all meet at the Light.

## We All Have a Connection to Spirits

When I released my first book, The Lee Avenue Haunting, it was received with a rather warm embrace, and I am very grateful for that. The outpouring of support I received, humbled me. There were so many e-mails letting me know that so many people out there have had similar experiences. They wanted me to know, I wasn't alone.

So for my next book, I wanted to take a special section, dedicate it to them, honor these lovely people, and let them share their experiences. They shared some vulnerable moments in their lives that profoundly changed the course of what they believed spiritually.

I would like to take this moment, to say thank you from the bottom of my heart, to all of you, for sharing these moments with me, and everyone else. It took courage that forever will be appreciated, and held in my heart.

So without further ado, I bring you the experiences, of those who reached out to me.

# SPIRITS AMONG US
## PART II

# CHAPTER ✌24✌

## THE HAUNTED ROCKER

It was February 6$^{th}$, 2013. I was driving home from work, it was around eight pm. It was cold, and the night sky, lit up every star. They were especially bright this particular evening. My car was running on empty, so I thought I would stop off and fill up on some gas at my local Sunoco gas station, in my home town of German Town, New York, about a mile from my home.

I had gotten out of the car, started to pump the gas, and I nodded to the attendant, as I was a regular customer. I noticed an SUV pull up adjacent to my car, but I really didn't turn around to look at the person. I just kept pumping my gas, and going about my business.

Then, I felt as if someone was looking at me. I turned around to look, casually, to see who was looking at me, and this woman was dead panning me and smiling. I smiled and nodded, and said "Hello." I noticed she was a well-dressed corporate type, mid-forties, long dark hair and she wore eye glasses.

I was finishing up pumping gas and getting ready to get back into my car when she blurted out something I was not expecting. She said, "Aren't you Ed Bates?" I was stunned … I had never seen this woman before in my life. How did she know me? I was blown away. Had she been waiting for me? What was the deal here? I was curious so I fed into it. "Yes … Yes I am Ed Bates." She said, "I see you on Facebook all the time and all your wonderful pictures that you take of the moon." Then it clicked for me, I said, "Ok, ok ok."

I laughed to myself, "It made sense now." I was worried that someone had been stalking me. She mentioned, "Oh you do that Ghost hunting too don't you?" I said, "Yes I do, with Poughkeepsie Paranormal. I love it! I seem to have a real, open flowing communication with the spirits and I just love all of them."

She then quipped, "Let's cut the small talk okay?" I was a little taken back by her boldness but I said, "Yes okay, what I can do for you." She seemed to know an awful a lot about me but I knew nothing about her. I had no idea where she was going with this whole thing. She pointed to the back of her SUV and said, "I have an old rocking chair I have been driving around with. It belonged to my grandmother. It is over eighty years old. I believe it's haunted. I have seen it move in my house and I want it out of my home. There used to be a life sized doll that sat in it. But I sold it on EBAY for four-hundred dollars."

I was immediately interested in having this chair. "Nothing scares me," I said to her. She said, "Good the chair is all yours!" She went to the back of the SUV and unlatched the hatch back part of it. She dragged it down and brought it over to me.

It was in pristine condition with the original upholstery, a floral pattern. There were no engravings on. No year that it was made. No nothing. I had only her word. She never shook my hand; she never gave me her name. She got into her SUV and pulled away fast.

As I was trying to fit this rocker into my Sedan, the gas station attendant ran out and asked if she had left money with me for the gas she pumped. I looked at him like no why would she leave it with me? She took off without paying.

So I began to wonder if it was a scam or if she was that scared about the chair. I got the chair home and brought it upstairs to my bedroom. I settled in for the night as I prepared my dinner and headed back to my bedroom to eat and watch one of my favorite shows called "Shipping Wars."

I figured as I watched the show I would set up my paranormal equipment on it to see if I can get any reading's on it. So I set up a K-2 meter which measures the electromagnetic fields. The higher the fields, the lights on the meters go from yellow to red. I also set up a sensor light facing the chair to capture if anything or anyone was to sit in the chair. I set up an infra-red video camera overnight so while that I slept it would catch any images moving about the chair if any.

I figured if this woman was telling me any truth, I mean she knew who I was, let me give her a chance to believe her. As I sat there watching television and eating my dinner I noticed out of the corner of my eye the bright red light lit right up. The K-2 was rested in the center of the seat of the rocker. My bedroom door started to push open. There was no one else home but my mother, who was on the first floor, resting on the couch.

I asked, "Do you like where I placed the chair?" At that, the sensor light went off as the door got pushed open a little more. This went on and on for another hour.

I would ask questions and the K-2 lights kept going to red after I would ask a question. I finally knew I had to go to bed, it was getting late. I was curious to see what the infra-red video would pick up by the next day. But I couldn't view it until the next night after work. So the whole day at work (I work at nursing home in Hudson, New York), I kept thinking about looking at my footage. I told my co-workers about it and they were amazed. The work day came to an end and I rushed home to review my findings.

I was shocked to see a shadow figure hovering around the chair at some points of the video, on and off throughout the night as I slept. I set up the K-2 meter once again and the sensor light began to flicker on and off throughout the night as I slept. I set up the K-2 meter once again and began to ask questions. I asked, "Are you that woman's grandmother?" The light went to red right away, then back down to yellow.

I really wished this woman had given me her contact information to speak with her. There was so much activity going on with this chair. I would of loved to help her some more, and not to mention she owes the Sunoco station some money.

Submitted by Edward Bates, Germantown, New York

Donna Parish-Bischoff

# CHAPTER ❧25❧

## SURROUNDED BY LOVE

There was a time in my life when I felt that I was at the end of my rope. Between my job, living expenses, relationship, and just life in general, all combined. I couldn't see any hope in sight, no matter which way I turned. I even had thoughts of suicide as an easy way out not knowing which way to turn, or who to turn to.

Then one night I got a spiritual sign from someone or something that was watching over me that night. I woke up in the middle of the night feeling like something was holding me down so I couldn't move. I saw what looked like angels with long flowing gowns circling over my bed. I felt very scared as to what was happening to me.

Being in a daze and not quite awake, I thought at first, it was a dream. Then I saw a glowing figure on my curtain in the shape of a small angel with its wings spread while the others continued to circle my bed as to guide me somewhere or protect me. I started to think that maybe I had died and they had come for me. Then all of a sudden I got a real peaceful feeling over my body and started to fall asleep, real peacefully, with a vision presented to me of a little boy holding a man's hand standing on a flat rock next to a lake.

I slept very calm and peaceful that night and woke up the next morning feeling very refreshed, and could remember everything from the night before. I never could figure out what the image was until recently when it hit me that it was I holding my dad's hand, when I was young standing on the rock, at my grandparent's summer cabin on Candlewood Lake, in CT.

I had many good times there over the years growing up and think that maybe the vision I had was to tell me that like before that I was safe holding my dad's hand back then and that God was holding my hand now and I was safe with him and everything will be all right again.

# Donna Parish-Bischoff

Submitted by John Boles, Red Hook, New York
Paranormal Investigator, Indy Para

# CHAPTER ✎26✎

## THE GOLD WATCH

I am young, indestructible, and I fear nothing. I have had no reason to be afraid—until today. At 20 years old, I never intimately experienced death. Today will be the day I feel an empty void in performing simple daily acts I had taken for granted. Silly things like going to lunch or parking my car in the mall parking lot would be unnerving. Today is the day that Jimmy, my co-worker, will run up to me and yell, "Oh my God, did you hear that John is dead?" My heart will sink to the floor, and I will want to barf right where I stand. My friend had died.

### Fast-forward Two Weeks

For weeks, my overactive brain continued reliving our last moments together. John and I were working hard in retail to save up for cars. We often talked about our dream hot rod of the week and simple things that were going on in our lives.

Going to work every day was painful. I had just lost my lunch buddy and a friend that I looked forward to seeing and chatting with daily. Not only was John my friend, but I had hoped our relationship would blossom into more. Our bond seemed to be headed in that direction, but never came to fruition. It was weeks of taunting, teasing, and harassing. You know, the things that future lovers do. Whenever, I saw him walk in my direction, my heart fluttered in my chest, and I would feel my face flush. *Did he notice? Sure, he did.*

Not knowing what the future held, I regarded our last moments together as insignificant. It hurt me to recall our conversations. The Christmas rush was bearing down on us, as customers hustled and bustled, in and out of the store getting their last minute shopping done. John causally moseyed into the shop and poked around the records, fussing with the loose gold watch on his wrist as he always did. I glanced up looking his way. His golden blonde wavy hair met the wire frames of his glasses. I could see that his brow was ruffled over his blue eyes. Our passing glances locked on each other. "What's your problem now?" I brazenly asked. "Ah, nothing," John said as he sped toward the door, "We'll talk about it later."

Those were the last words I would ever hear him speak. My mind raced crafting ridiculous guesses as to what he was going to say. The guilt I felt was almost too much to bear. There was no excuse for not making an appearance at his funeral. I didn't know any of his friends or family and didn't understand the protocol for such things. Each day I drove to work, my eyes couldn't help but focus in the direction of *John's private parking space*. I was yearning for someone to tell me this was all a mistake, and I would see his car parked in the corner lot.

Later that evening, while in a sound sleep, I rolled over and noticed the golden glow of a light shining through the door of the living room. "Oh. Damn! I left the light on again," I moaned. I yanked myself to an upright position and noticed the luminosity of the light began to change. I rubbed my eyes and tried to shake myself conscious. The glow continued to materialize into the form of a man sitting on the arm of my couch. *What the hell?* I thought to myself. I could not believe what I was seeing. The more I stared at the glow, the more defined it became. Then I saw the glimmer of a gold watch. Our faces met, and the glow slowly faded out my front door. I felt both serene and freaked out at the same time.

## Thirty Years Later

I have always carried some sense of guilt for not officially saying goodbye to my friend, and I often think of John—wondering about what could have been. I feel that the event that occurred in my living room was paranormal. It was a sign from John telling me not to worry. I am ok, and I told you I would talk to you later!

John's death was violent and pointless. John's story has always disturbed me. Wanting to gain closure over this tragic event, I began to write about haunted history to share stories with others who have similar interests. I connected with a colleague who also had a paranormal experience. I excitedly shared my story. To my shock, my colleague was friends with John, and knew where he was buried. Was this message from beyond the grave?

I got to pay my respects after thirty years.

Submitted by Donna Davies, New York
Halloween Author & Halloween Artist

Donna Parish-Bischoff

# CHAPTER ᎒27᎒

### THE MAN IN THE TOP HAT

It was summertime, in 1977. A group of teenagers were 'hanging out down by the river'. It was the Hudson River in north Riverdale, Bronx, NY, a favorite nighttime spot to stargaze and have fun. As dusk was approaching, several of us at first, and then later, all of us, noticed a large square-shaped flat "thing" with lights aligned under the bottom of it, hovering over the George Washington Bridge, and then moving slowly toward where we were, remaining in the air over the river for approximately thirty minutes.

Suddenly it disappeared without us seeing where it went. A few minutes later a man appeared where we were, although he was a bit closer to the banks of the river. He appeared to be dressed in old-fashioned clothing, although he did not look old. He had a long white beard and was wearing a top hat. He was definitely not dressed in contemporary clothing but something more like out of the pages of a history book.

He didn't approach us or say anything, but he did stop in front of us; it seemed as if he could not relate to us and would not face us completely. He then skipped by, yes, skipped, in a flamboyant fashion as he passed us. He proceeded toward a wooded area.

Some of the boy's in our group ran after him to only report he had disappeared. We all talked about it, and everyone present witnessed the same oddity. It seemed as if he was a visitor from some other time perhaps?

Some of us felt it he had something to do with the "flat ship," and he somehow landed by us and then was whisked back off.

I will never forget this incident, and although strange, I was not afraid of him, just curious.

# Donna Parish-Bischoff

Submitted by Lorraine Ferrissey: Yonkers, New York

# CHAPTER ❧28❧

## NIGHTY NIGHT, SLEEP TIGHT

My grandmother lived with us for a period of time. Since we shared a bed, I was used to the feeling of someone getting in and out of the bed long after I had gotten in bed and settled in for the night. Some month's later she had moved out, I got a room of my very own, and I had a double bed at this point.

It was late one night and I was lying down on my side. I had not been in bed long enough to have fallen asleep. Actually, I wasn't even sleepy yet. Behind me, the bed suddenly was weighed down as if someone had gotten into the bed with me, and I felt my body roll back and forth involuntarily in response to movement of the weight. I became so startled I just rolled the covers up and over my head, and almost passed out from fright. I literally felt scared to death. I didn't know what to do.

My grandmother was still alive at the time this occurred so I cannot attribute this to her. Until this day I have no clue whose ghostly presence that was.

Submitted by: Lisa Fredericks, New Hampshire
Lisa was eight years old at the time of this experience.

Donna Parish-Bischoff

# CHAPTER ∽29∾

## FOR WHOM THE BELL TOLLS

My best paranormal experience was heard by all that were in my house at the time.

My soul mate, and friend, MaryAnn would visit me in the mornings, and lean against my doorbell. Having it constantly ring she used to say she wanted to make sure I was awake. MaryAnn had become ill and passed away. I felt devastated.

We moved into this house in Yorktown Height's to have a fresh start. It was a holiday. Maybe Memorial Day or Labor Day. My son was here, as well as my husband, and my granddaughter.

Out of nowhere, my doorbell started to ring. Just as if my friend were here and leaning up against the doorbell joking around with me. I went to the front door. No one was there. We went to the back door no one was here. My husband who knows that Maryann used to do this to me yelled out, "Hey Mare, stop." However it did not stop, and believe it or not, even when my husband disconnected the bell, it still rang.

I know that was her. She said she would come back to haunt me, (In a good way of course!) I loved her very much.

Now here is some of the other stuff that goes on here!

My dogs normally sit by the gate looking into the dark dining room. Sometimes that is all they do, sit and stare, or sometimes, they will stand on all fours, ears up with their tails wagging. It's amazing. I wish I knew who they are seeing. My dad passed away last year, and he would stay with us a lot. I have heard him walking around upstairs right over our family room, a few times.

My house is very much awake with this activity, and I love every bit of it to be honest. I feel close to my loved ones.

# Donna Parish-Bischoff

Submitted by: Ann Golino, Yorktown Heights, New York

# CHAPTER ❧30❧

## IT ALL STARTED SOMEWHERE

Which came first? Spirit before the human? Logically, does it even matter? Perhaps to a bunch of scientists that spent dozens of years stuffed around tables and books arguing with one another. Sure. To a religious regime because it would overturn everything we ever learned it to be. Of course, I understand.

But does it really matter when all we all are, deep down inside is spirit? In spirit form and human form to me I feel connected. Doesn't matter that we can't always see them or hear them. They are there.

But does it really matter? When all we all are deep down inside is spirit? Right? In spirit form and in human form, I feel connected. Does it matter that we can't always see them or hear them? They are there.

Same difference as if a loved one lived on the other side of the world. You don't seen them or speak to them all the time, but sometimes communicate through a frequency, wires, and electricity. At the end it all comes down to technology.

I feel there are endless realms of existence, like a spiral effect. For some downward, and others upward. It's part of our evolution in the spirit world. Each day whether a living being, or in spirit form we live and learn lessons. I do believe this to be so.

As living beings, when our bodies are at rest our subconscious has the capabilities of visiting wonderful places and learning great lessons. Our brains are like a candy store to the cosmos when we go to sleep at night. We reach planes of existence, that in the waking hours, we had no clue that they ever existed.

Haven't you ever wondered why the human brain cannot be used more than ten percent? But yet tap into your Pineal Gland (third eye) and you will feel a vibration, a wave, a happening to your subconscious that you have never felt before. This will allow you to explore these Realms and delve deeper into the unknown to know your spirit better.

Sure there is the noise of the day, traffic, bills to pay, bosses to answer to, kid's to feed, houses to clean. But at the end of the day when you put your head down, your spirit flies over the rooftops and into the universe of dreams, and when that happens, wouldn't you like to harness that a bit and take something back when you wake up and learn more from yourself by morning's light? I know what my answer would be.

It is up to us to be open to this wonderful gift, accepting of these lessons, and use these lessons in the waking hours. I was taught that a long time ago when I met a man named Craig Junjulas. I was fourteen years old at the time, my friend Rose was his neighbor. She told me all about him and I was intrigued to meet him and speak to him.

He went on to become one of what I consider a leading spiritual teacher in the world. He now resides in Sedona, Arizona and travels between there, and Japan teaching. In the years that followed his teachings, about the subconscious, and how much we can soak up, and the places we can visit while our physical bodies were asleep rung in my ears.

If you really think about it, our bodies are endless miracles. Our brains, our spirits, the science that ties and binds it altogether. And it's all quite beautiful like a blooming garden. All the discoveries you will notice as you walk through the gates of your own venture. So whether you think it's sheer spiritual, or science—it's both, together, hand in hand, that brought it all here today, because without neither of these I could not sit here and share my thoughts with you.

Donna Parish-Bischoff, Hyde Park, New York

# CHAPTER ❧31❧

MANSIONS IN THE SKY
(A VISIT FROM LARRY)

It was April 8th, 2011, I had awoken from a very vivid dream. It was a few weeks short of a year of my brothers' death. I had been missing him, as I still do and will always. I still hear his voice in my head. The familiar, "Hey Donna," that upbeat, positive, everything will be alright outlook he carried.

Sometimes I think our brains create a landscape in which we play and feel safe. A bubble of security, love, peace. A place where time means nothing and we have everything we ever needed. But in this particular dream it was different. It was too real for even words to do it justice, I will try though.

I had been standing outside on a lawn of a beautiful, French looking mansion. I slowly approached its doors and entered in. As I wandered inside, I noticed the long windows that were ornamented with yellow drapes with large navy blue stripes. They were balloon style drapes with tie-backs allowing the bright sun to burst through. In front of the windows were rounded off half tables with tall vases holding fresh cut wild flowers in which the scent was aromatic and sweet. Upon entering another large room I had taken notice to a monstrous sky light that drew out the natural tones of the hard wood flooring allowing a warm tone to illuminate the natural of the wood. French provincial furniture adorned what had been a sitting room of some form. I was in complete and total awe as I just took it all in.

I was really just enjoying this place so much I had no questions of where I was. I did not care. I felt at peace. I began hearing laughter in the distance coming from another room. I began to follow it with a natural curiosity. I soon located this room. It had this massive indoor, heated pool. You could actually see the steam rising from the water as people were splashing around in it and really enjoying themselves.

Laughter echoed throughout the place and happiness was abundant. Around the parameters of the pool were bistro style tables and chairs set up with checkered table cloths draped over the tops of the tables. There were people seated and having a great time, laughing it up and feasting. It seemed like a great party I did not want to leave.

I walked into another room and I saw small circles of people gathered and chatting and laughing and holding drinks and plates of food smiling. And all of a sudden, there he was! My brother Larry! Looking so handsome and smiling, healthy, happy. I said, "The place looks great!"

He said, "Yeah, Gerry decorated it!" Gerry is my sister in law, who is still very much with us. He gestured with his hands and said, "Look around, have a good time." He pointed in the direction of the kitchen. I shook my head yes like I agreed.

I started to walk towards the kitchen. I noticed there was a huge bay window. I could see a petting zoo through it. My brother knows I love animals so he sent me where he knew where I would go! Hmmm. Clever man he is! I saw the exotic birds, goats, alpacas, and pigs. I ran out there to all of them like a moth to a flame because I love, love, love animals! I noticed a corn field. I started to walk through it, and then suddenly it turned to a muddy field, and as I looked behind me the mansion had vanished, the animals were gone. I heard no more laughter.

The alarm went off next to my bed and I awoke, but I honestly believe I had a visit with the other side as I was allowed a glimpse of what it's like and how my brother is doing. I was worried about him. I believe he wanted me to not worry about him any longer. Although I no longer worry about him, I still miss him. Was it a dream? Or a visit? You decide? I know what I think.

Donna Parish-Bischoff, Hyde Park, New York

# CHAPTER ❧32❧

## MEETING CRAIG JUNJULAS

I met Craig Junjulas, metaphysical teacher, clairvoyant, author and lecturer who now lives in Sedona, Arizona, when I was fourteen years old through my friend, Rose. At the time, he was her neighbor, in Yonkers, New York. My friend Rose knew of all the strange and bizarre things I had been through in my short fourteen year's. She explained to me that Craig was studying the metaphysical, and was a parapsychologist. She felt perhaps he may be able to shed some light or assist me with what I was going through.

She made an appointment with him one day after we got home from high school, to sit with him. His mother was home, and brought us tea and cake, and she had such a sweet smile. Then she left the three of us in the living room to discuss what I had been through with Lee Avenue, and everything else I had experienced.

For whatever reason, I have residual energy that bounces off of me. Those certain types of things happen to me, around me, because of me, etc. He said it was common because of my age, being an adolescent. He said, "It comes with the territory," and smiled. He said that often enough, teens throw off an energy that replicates a poltergeist activity. The thing here was to channel my energy another way to try and fine tune it. Try and meditate, and increase the power of the brain, and bring down my higher self, to guide me through. He said that everyone is capable of harnessing those powers but sadly, we don't know it, and push the power away in denial.

Meeting Craig that afternoon was an eye opener of all three of my eyes. I was so happy to meet him, and I must say when you are in his presence you feel a great sense of peace, and you walk away feeling as if you can do anything. He moved to Arizona and created a wonderful world to explore and help others just the way he was meant to.

He travels constantly, teaching, but I was lucky enough to catch up with him to get an interview and shed some insight on what he feels regarding some topics. I will provide where you can reach him, his website, contact information, and the books he has written here. If you ever get a chance to see him in person, tell him Donna sent you, and tell him I said hello.

Here is his website: http://higherselfdiscovery.com. You will be able to contact him on that link for his e-mail, contact phone number, his calendar of upcoming classes, and what state he will be in. The following are the books he has published: *Psychic Tarot*, *IAN The Boy*, and *Aquarian Tarot Deck with Book*. Stay connected because he has more to follow!

Submitted by Donna Parish-Bischoff, Hyde Park, New York

Photo courtesy of Craig Junjulas

# CHAPTER ❧33❧

AN INTERVIEW WITH
CRAIG JUNJULAS

I was so honored that he agreed to be a part of my book, and I am proud to say he is a part of my life, my spiritual journey, and the path I chose to take, rather than some other path a troubled teen with problems might have chosen. I say, "Thank you Craig, much love to my spiritual brother."

**At what age did you notice this awareness, this higher vibration of *higher self-discovery*?**

My mother told me that I was a happy child and would hang out with the dog in my playpen. I don't remember details, but remember feeling a special relationship and ability to have a basic communion/communication with animals, bugs, trees, clouds, and most things in nature. Being the youngest child, I was able to commune with nature spirits while my older siblings were in school. It was not until I took psychic development classes that I realized how aware of the invisible world I was as a child.

Kindergarten was when I experienced the shutting down of my natural higher senses and my emotions in order to replace them with what my parents, teachers, and fellow students expected of me. I don't know how young I was when it was clear that I was different from most other people around me, but I remember being told over and over that I was too sensitive, or that I had an overactive imagination, whenever I tried to explain to others things that I witnessed, like fairies and ghosts.

**Did you try and run from these feeling's or shut them down and deny them?**

My natural tendency was to explore these feelings and investigate their meanings. I would stare into clouds, still water, candle flames, rocks, etc. in order to see differently and feel a mystical connection. I would lie on the grass for a long time staring deeply into the blades of grass until I could see the little people that were invisible, and until my eyes adjusted, and my imagination came into focus. I learned not to tell my parents too much because the answer to my visions was that it was only my imagination and I would be in trouble if I did not shut up and go to sleep.

Their answer to my hearing voices would be that you have to go to the doctor if it continued. If I shared it with my siblings, they did not want to encourage this behavior because they knew that it would lead me into trouble with the adult world. Finally, as I approached my teen years, I searched for ways to dull these feelings with alcohol, cigarettes, and whatever else made me seem more like the people around me.

**What would you suggest to those that are interested in getting in touch with their *higher-selves*? Is there an intermediate way to start that would not be intimidating?**

Just as you get better at dancing, playing music, singing, painting, writing, and other creative things, the more you practice the easier it becomes. I have a few basic techniques on my website that can bring the person to a point of readiness gently and gradually. We are always connected to our higher selves. It is like a flashlight shining down on the earth but we only notice the spot that hits our brain and we do not invite it more deeply into our bodies. Getting in touch with our Higher Selves is like getting in touch with a loving parent, or an old friend that longs to reconnect with you. Just call and they will be there for you – but you have to make the time and space to hang out with them intimately.

There are three basic steps to most spiritual development systems

1. Relax
2. Energize, and,
3. Connect to a higher source.

The more you practice relaxing the mind (expanding awareness) and relaxing the body (progressive relaxation techniques) the easier it is to connect because you are becoming less dense and existing in an expanded form much more like spiritual beings exist. You are shifting into a higher vibration like helium balloon that was compressed and stuck in the mud at the bottom of a lake and now rises through the water and floats up into the air.

The second step allows energy to flow through your body with less resistance, meaning less pain and more pleasure. If you think of yourself as a dense physical body, it becomes a tight container that resists the flow of energy. Even someone saying nice words to you can hurt as it tries to pass through you body and flow through your somewhat tight and defensive heart. If you practice opening your aura, by thinking of yourself as a 12 foot ball of energy you are making room for energy and making a nice large container for your higher self to fit into. If you also think of your physical body as being pure energy, you can use your creative thinking (imagination) to redesign yourself as having a system that has open highways for energy to flow through. You can feel warm and fluffy and able to conduct powerful energies without resistance. Opening the seven chakras (energy centers) and releasing old dense energy patterns built up from years of fears, worries and doubts is a part of this opening process.

The third step is simple. Sit in a quiet space with an open mind and send out a request for connection, guidance and protection. You will feel warmth, an expansive feeling, a flow of pleasant energy, or other sensations in your body as you become more aware of your higher self's presence. As you continue to practice, your mind becomes more enlightened and your body more illuminated.

**Do you feel everyone has this within himself or herself?**

Yes. We all have the capacity to bring our higher selves deeper into our everyday lives. Some people try to remain shut down and hang onto being like others around them and do not allow the transformation until they experience a profound life crisis, as I did. I was in my mid-twenties working in science and suffering in a marriage that was toxic to both parties. My physical symptoms led me to doctors, who suggested psychotherapy, which opened me up in an explosive way. That led me to hypnotherapy and meditation, which led me to personal growth classes and psychic and spiritual development workshops followed.

**Describe what a *mansion world* is briefly.**

Although it means different things to different people, to describe it in terms that would be easy to understand, he would say it is a *belief system.*

A mansion world is a level of reality above the physical plane. When you meditate, and free yourself of the limiting beliefs of the physical body being a closed container, you can venture out into the mansion worlds while semi-awake. We travel into other dimensions every night while we sleep. A person developing their higher awareness begins to travel while retaining a sense of their earth consciousness. A general view would be that the mansion worlds are a series of realities that shift into higher frequencies and advanced states of consciousness and are dedicated to the elevation of beings toward superior realization of the true essence of creation and the Creator. Each planet, star system, and galaxy offer different types of life forms and forms of development due to the physical properties of the planet and the non-physical levels that envelop the planet and the surrounding area. Each world, from the newly born star to the planets and stars involved in the crashing together of two galaxies, are overseen by loving beings dedicated to the welfare and evolution of the spirits existing there. Locally, the earth has higher levels of energy that we can access and spiritual guiding beings assisting us with our individual ascension. Ascended Masters (Jesus, Buddha, Quan Yin, St. Germaine, etc.) are humans who have displayed these elevated ways of existence while living in human bodies, then shift upward to live in the mansion worlds to continue teaching and helping us to rise.

**What is the most significant sign you have experienced to date, feel free to include more than one if you wish. To date, from your higher self, what has been life changing or remarkable that you can recall?**

When I was first beginning to develop my psychological and psychic awareness, the "signs" were much needed and very helpful in assisting me to find and remain on my Spiritual path. Much like highway signs when driving to a new location. But, after a while I needed less and less external signs, just like returning to a familiar town requires less attention to signage. Although not a momentary phenomenon, I would have to say that the gradual and continuous building up of the sense of being more "connected" to my spiritual guides and Higher Self has been the best long term experience as well as the most life changing. Every time I do a demonstration in which I channel my spiritual guides in a class or satsang, I feel a shift, a deepening of my resolve to continue my search for truth and share my findings with those who are earnestly seeking.

As far as discussing significant event, I would say that the first meditations that I ever performed were the most momentous and life changing. I was around 26 years old, still in psychotherapy sessions trying to reconcile my unique abilities with what the people around me expected from me. I was trying to be the type of husband that was expected of me and the type of obedient corporate worker that the rest of the scientific researchers seemed to be able to act like on a regular basis.

I did not formally believe in anything metaphysical at the time. I was given a book, *Relaxation Response* (Benson) that broke Transcendental Meditation (TM) down into scientific understanding. I repeated the number "one" over and over in my head and imagined a golden number "1" flying out into space and disappearing into the fields of stars until I was not in the room as the meditator anymore. I found myself floating and kneeling before a being that was sitting on a throne. He was glowing so brightly that I could not raise my eyes to see his face. It was like trying to gaze directly at the sun. I remember seeing sandaled feet. Other beings were standing around and behind the throne looking at me. They too had shining faces. The person on the throne spoke to me for a while, but I could not remember what was said to me after I returned from the meditation, but had a sense that it was worth the effort of repairing myself and trying to discover who I really was inside the confused jangle of thoughts and emotions. I only remember hearing his voice telling me to return to the earth and heal my brothers and sisters. So, I am still a work in progress and travel into other dimensions whenever the need arises. On rare occasions I have returned to this place over the years.

I have been visited by my deceased father on a few occasions over the past 30 plus years. I have sat next a dying patient and helped a few people cross over. Other significant events were when receiving regressive hypnotherapy or performing guided journeys to travel into the past to explore and heal my own past lives. Each time I do so, a significant shift in my present life usually occurs and makes my everyday life much better.

**I write about my brother in this book and how he visited me. I asked you to read the chapter and analyze it for me, to explain exactly what you think happened to my  levels of consciousness. Please comment.**

It is difficult to analyze and define such a broad and emotionally laced series of events that have such strong family, and past life ties. But, you have had the inclination and the courage to constantly challenge yourself, and search for the truth regardless of how difficult it was to experience in the moment, and how long the haunting process of recognition, acceptance, and release of prior beliefs, and personal judgment took. I have an image of you healing a client, closing your eyes and going on a journey. Descending into hell, walking through fire, walking up to the Prince of Darkness and standing with your hands defiantly on your hips and telling him to release the soul of your client or you are going to tell his father on him. So, I guess you have always had the courage to research, experiment, explore, and apply what you have learned to help create a therapeutic system for others to use to make their lives better. Through many lifetimes you have searched, even if you were mocked, cast out of social circles, tarred and feathered, killed. You keep returning and trying to help.

You had to fight through the personal grief of losing your brother while simultaneously being forced to face the truth of his death, and keeping your mind open, and your psychic senses active. Shutting down and falling into a pit of depression, and disbelief is a much easier path. You had to try to reconcile your personal life's sense of pain and suffering, with the desire to discover the truth behind all things, and continue to offer comfort and healing to others. You used the techniques that you had practiced over the years, to help you open to the higher dimensions, in order to remain connected with your brother. Therefore, you were able to have a wonderful moment of union after his physical body was gone. This event can sure you up in amazing ways in the future because you were given *personal proof* of the hereafter. It will also help you to remain resolved, when helping others who are suffering in the future, as you move forward into the world as a healer.

Submitted by Donna Parish-Bischoff,
Hyde Park, New York

---

*I would like to thank Craig Junjulas to take the time he did with me to explore the unknown once. I truly appreciate your gifts that you have given all of us.*

# CHAPTER ᵔ34ᵔ

## THE PUMPKIN AND THE CHAP STICK

This happened to me, I believe it is true. Though I have experienced tragedy, it made me know without doubt that there is a spirit world. An experience happened. I have knowledge of something that's not supposed to exist. It's not something you can talk about to everyone; few people in my life know this.

In June 2004, my boyfriend Rob died in a construction accident, in Austerlitz, Columbia County, NY. He was a builder working on new house construction, it was a hot summer day, he was dehydrated, and apparently fainted according to the coroner's report, falling from up near the roof, landing in the basement area.

Still alive, unconscious, when airlifted to Albany Med, he died two days later. I last saw him with his eyes closed on life support. I would never see him again. I asked him if he would keep his promise to me; that if one of us died, we would come back if it was possible in some way. At the time, this was an agreement my mother and I had. I didn't really think such a thing was possible.

His death was so devastating to me. I had been married before, but he was really the person for me. I was just lost after he died, it broke my heart. Up to two weeks after he passed, I would sometimes find things moved in my house, like a pair of earrings his mother gave me from Lake George. At first I just dismissed it, until, that same pair of earrings, along with the bottle of his sunburn lotion that I had put on him just days before he died, were in the middle of my bed one morning. As I walked into the doorway and saw that, it literally took my breath away, stopped me in my tracks. It's like this overwhelming feeling of peace, I cried at the same time, it seemed unbelievable, yet it was right there, I lived alone.

One night, while reading a book in my bed for most of the evening, my female yellow lab Skye, looked sharply over her shoulder, and jumped off the bed. The only time that she ever did that was when Rob walked in the room because he didn't like her on my bed. The candles in my room were also flickering and making noise like a hissing sound. The candles I hadn't noticed right away while reading, but the dog's behavior made me wonder.

About two weeks after he died, I was starting to have somewhat normal days. I was coming out of a store one day, and really for once, not thinking about him at all that day as I was preparing to go to a cookout later at a friend's house, and feeling actually happy. All of a sudden, to my right, I heard someone say, "Hey babe,", and I looked over towards the car wash thinking there was someone there. But there was no one outside around me at all. It was still and quiet, like it was within arm's reach, to my right, and I heard it, plain as day. It wasn't Rob's voice as I knew it, but almost like someone speaking in a tin can, that's what it sounded like, and he used to call me babe. I stood there for a minute looking around thinking, "How could I have just heard that?" That was the last unusual thing to happen for a while.

Six months after he died, I was sort of back to normal. I was starting to be Ok with the fact that he was gone and never coming back. A psychic was giving a talk to 20 people at a bookstore quite far away. I decided to go. I went with a friend. I didn't really believe in this sort of thing.

After the talk, she offered me a brief reading. Before I went up to her, I felt that she would have to tell me something about Rob, or in my mind, she was not real. I asked her if I would ever hear from Rob again. Puzzled at first, she asked, "He isn't in his corporal body." I said, "Yes, he's dead." Then she said, "Well, he's around you more than you realize. When you're with your dog, he moves things to get your attention because you do not realize he's there." She also described him perfectly; as a waffly person, a bit messy, who starts a lot of projects and didn't finish them.

This was two counties away from home, there's no way she could have known any of this, and she had my attention, and everyone else's. She told me, "Someone is coming for you. He will be someone who HELPS you," and just when she says that, my friend steps forward, and he's smiling, she says, "He wants you to be happy." I do not cry in public, but she had me in tears. I was embarrassed, and I really didn't know what to think. I was starting to think that there really is a spirit world.

A year later, I sold my house, and rented a new house. I had a new Labrador, a one year old male, Saxon, who I was training with hand signals. I went outside to bring my Labrador in. While I was outside, I met a roofer who was working on the house next door. He walked up to us, and my dog that normally would start to get aggressive at seeing a stranger, especially near me, uncharacteristically did nothing, he was calm. This was not lost on me, and I thought it really strange but I felt safe.

We developed a casual friendship, where we exchanged pleasantries, and he would later help me in significant ways, such as helping me move out of that rented house. He took nothing from me, and we really barely knew each other. We would often cross paths, and from the time I met him, he was always working within two blocks from me, either right next door, or behind my house. It was a bit baffling to me. I had developed a crush on him, but he was married.

Two years later, he was working on the house next door, leaving the job, it was Halloween day. He called me over and asked if I would move my car, a dumpster was arriving. On the sidewalk in front of the house, standing next to each other, I felt like I had to keep looking over my shoulder, I felt this sort of breeze. I felt weird, and didn't understand it. I don't remember any of the words the roofer said at all, because I couldn't pay attention to him.

The roofer left, I went inside to take a nap, but out of the corner of my eye, saw something amiss. One pumpkin previously on the wide windowsill was now on the floor several feet away in front of the fireplace. Next to it was my chap stick, which had been on the table several feet away. There was just no way these items could've gotten there, rolled there, or anything, I lived alone, was outside for maybe ten minutes. The significance of the pumpkin was obvious to me, as Halloween had been my first date with Rob. The Chap Stick didn't make sense to me until much, much, later in the day, when in my mind, I re-lived that first date, and how we sat in a dark movie theatre on Halloween, and he kissed me for the first time, leaned back, licked his lips and asked me if I was wearing Chap Stick, the same kind that was now on the floor near the pumpkin.

Hard to describe and it gave me chills, made me cry. A lot of things just started to make sense. The things that moved, what the psychic said, my dog. All these signs. Even if you tried to dismiss them, they were unbelievable coincidences.

Donna Parish-Bischoff

Submitted By: Lisa LaMonica, Hudson New York

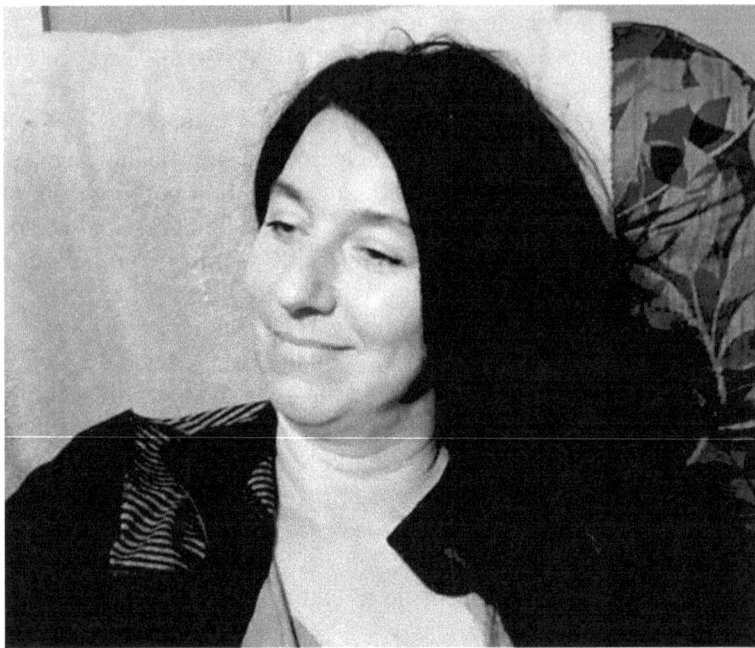

# CHAPTER ❧35❧

## A GIFT FROM BEYOND

My most memorable experience happened in 2009, when my boyfriend's childhood friend died unexpectedly at the age of thirty. In the days following his death, a lot of people were receiving sign's from him. My experience happened within a day or two after his passing.

I was on my way to work and I stopped at a gas station to purchase a newspaper specifically for his obituary. I got out of my car and locked all of the doors. I was in and out of the gas station within three minutes. When I returned to my car, a gold cross necklace that I had hanging off my rearview mirror was now tied in a knot around my steering wheel.

I sat there for a really long time so stunned that this had happened. I took a picture of it with my cell phone. I ended up calling my boyfriend's mother because I just could not figure out any other way this could have taken place.

I ended up giving the gold cross to the mother of the deceased friend. His mother felt as if that was a good sign that he was letting everyone know that he was okay and he did not want anyone to worry about him.

Submitted By Kelly Liebermann,
Wappingers Falls, New York

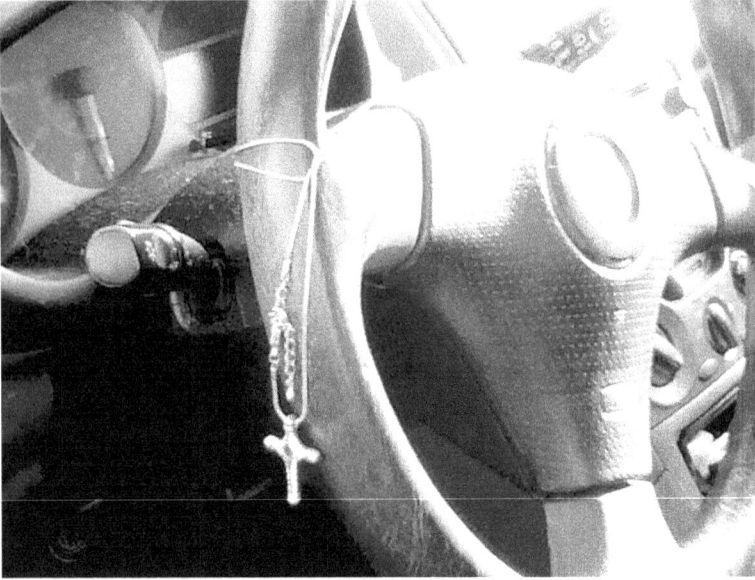

# CHAPTER ~36~

## SOMEONE TO WATCH OVER ME

It was around 1966; Arra Mowry was eleven years old when she encountered her very first experience with something bigger than all of us. It was then she knew there was something more out there in this universe co-existing right along the side of us. Here is her story:

Life as I knew it was steadily improving for me. My health improved to a point where I no longer needed to be a stay at home kid. I was able to spend my summers with my grandparents, who at the time lived in Fairfield, Ct. My Mom Mom and Pop Pop lived in a duplex house with my cousins living right next door. My Aunt and Uncle were divorced, with my Uncle living with my grandparents and my oldest cousin was adopted by my grandparents. That left my Aunt and her remaining 5 kids living immediately next door.

I became very good friends with my cousin Ricky, who was considerably younger than me, but we just hit it off. We were inseparable. My Aunt would take us places that were fun and entertaining, and this one weekday, we went to the beach, Jones Beach, on the Long Island Sound. I was a healthy swimmer, but mostly in swimming pools, I did not have much experience in lakes, creeks, ponds, or oceans.

I went out swimming this day and found myself getting pulled underwater. I'm assuming this was the undertow that they talk about. I was getting pulled further and further out and deeper and deeper underwater and was unable to get to the surface. While under the water, I felt panic and tried to think how I could save myself, because I knew I was going to drown.

I could see many little holes on the ocean floor and for a brief moment was wondering what they were and what sort of creature would pop out of there. As I was watching these holes, I remember swallowing more and more sea water until I knew this was the end. I can honestly say, at that point, I had a moment of peace and all panic left me. I was comfortable in concentrating on the holes on the ocean floor. No, I didn't see a bright light, and no, I didn't see my deceased relatives. I can only remember a sudden yank on my back and before I knew it, I was on the surface and could see the shoreline.

I started swimming towards the shore until I was able to touch the ocean floor and walk the rest of the way in. I was crying quite a bit and coughing pretty badly. Lots of water was coming out of me with each and every cough.

Was this my guardian angel? Perhaps the divine intervention of my Lord and Savior Jesus Christ or perhaps His Father?

I don't know who saved my life that morning but for that I am truly thankful.

Submitted by: Arra Mowry, Wappingers New York<br>
Author, Case Manager and Paranormal Investigator for<br>
Poughkeepsie Paranormal

Arra Mowry & Chloe

# CHAPTER ᦉ37ᦉ

### DON'T MESS WITH NANNY DAVE

In the 1970's, my girlfriend and I took a trip to Atlantic City. I spent many a summer there because a vast majority of my maternal family lived there in the small, little town of Pleasantville, NJ. My family also founded the other towns of Leeds Point and Somers Point.

We received an invitation to stay with my great Aunt Hattie and her daughter, Barbara. They lived in a beautiful old Victorian home on Main Street, in Pleasantville, NJ. It was in this two-story home, that most of my family had lived, and died in. The main living room served as a funeral home for deceased family members as well as friends around town. The house also acted as a birthing place, for the local midwives. Walking in from the back door, you would enter into a huge country style kitchen, with many windows throughout. Stepping through the kitchen, you would walk into a small dining room. At that time, my cousin Barbara used it as a bedroom. Her heart health issues would not permit her to walk much, and she certainly could not do stairs. Moving on to the right exit of the dining room, there is one of those famous long hallways leading to the typical monstrous front door. Turn left from the front door and you will walk into the formal living room, where the funerals took place. My aunt had recently had a double hip replacement so she was laid up in a hospital bed in that room. After climbing up over twenty-four steps to the second floor, you walk into a wonderful full sized bathroom. Now if you make a 180 turn to the right, the first room would be a small corner bedroom where I would sleep while visiting with my grandparents. In its day, this was the birthing room, but now my cousin Barbara used it as her sewing room. Moving down there is the master bedroom where my great grandparents slept. Because of the separate twin beds, it reminded me of I Love Lucy. On this visit, this is where my girlfriend and I slept. Continuing down the hallway there were two more bedrooms. These were all kid's rooms, where my cousins and other guests would stay.

To set the scenario, it was the middle of summer. Temperatures were in the neighborhood of 110 degrees during the day and low 100's during the night. We came back from a long day on the Atlantic City Boardwalk, taking in shows, sightseeing, and of course, shopping. We brought homemade ice cream from the infamous Kirstedders (not sure of the correct spelling) for my aunt and cousin. We enjoyed the ice cream, and my cousin Barbara told me that they were ready for bed and would suggest we do the same. Well, 9pm was not my idea of a good time for bed, but, since we were guests, we went upstairs. The room was so hot so we opened the windows but could only crack them about four inches. We were betting on the circulation of air from those windows by leaving the bedroom door open. As we sat there, we were discussing the oddities of the room next door, you know, the birthing room. The door was closed, and locked from the inside. To top things off, it was nailed shut from the inside. The nail tips were protruding into the hallway. Someone nailed the door shut from the inside. But how did they leave? Did someone do this, and live in that room, and was dead in there? Did they lock up this room this way and climb out the window down to the ground? We pondered some answers but nothing realistic came to mind. So we were sitting on the beds wondering just how the hell we were going to sleep in the heat and we got goofy. At that moment, Barbara yelled up from the bottom of the staircase informing us that we were making too much noise and they couldn't sleep. After apologizing, we continued talking in lower voices. We got to giggling and once again, Barbara yelled up announcing that if we don't keep it down she will have Nanny Dave come in. I apologized and giggled under my breath. My girlfriend asked who Nanny Dave was and I told her it was my great grandmother, who had died a thousand years ago. This went on with only a couple more warnings and without notice, an image appeared in the doorway. This image was faceless and extremely tall which the tiniest of heads. The image appeared to be floating with no apparent feet. It had on a long white gown, like dress, and then, disappeared as fast as it appeared. I looked at my girlfriend who saw it as well and asked, "What the hell was that?" We both were a little on edge but decided to shrug it off. As we both were lying down on the beds facing the doorway, my eyes were closed but something told me to open them and there it was again. I turned back around cautiously to look at my girlfriend her eyes were bulging. Obviously she saw it too. Again, we just quietly stayed there hoping it would leave.

When it happened a third time, I slowly looked back, and saw my girlfriend up and packing. I knew then this was the end of our visit. Of course, it was in the middle of the night so we got home by dawn. My mother asked why we were home so early, I explained what had happened. When I described the image we saw, she turned white. It seems that Nanny Dave, whom she had known, was close to seven feet tall and wore her hair in a bun, which made her face extremely small.

Was what we saw truly Nanny Dave? I don't know. But we know we saw an apparition of some sort.


Submitted By:
Arra Mowry, Wappingers Falls, Author, Case Manager and
Paranormal Investigator for Poughkeepsie Paranormal

Donna Parish-Bischoff

# CHAPTER 38

## DO DREAMS COME TRUE?

To set the stage, my parents lived in Sharon, Ct., up in Sharon Mountain. It was quite desolate up there, but they did befriend a younger couple who lived around the corner. The husband was actually the contractor that built my parents' home. I don't have permission to use their names, so I will call them "Bob and Mary."

Bob and Mary had recently purchased an old farmhouse up in Montgomery County, NY. Their house was also close to the home of my girlfriends parents. On weekends, Bob and Mary would go up to this house they just purchased to renovate it. My parents, my girlfriend, and I were invited up to Bob and Mary's house for a visit, and then onto my girlfriend's parents' house for dinner.

A few days earlier, while sleeping (of course!), I had this very vivid dream. The dream started with me walking up to this big white house with two white pillars in front. The landscaping was just lovely and the weather was a bright, sunny beautiful spring day. Evidently, I was going to this home for a visit. As I approached the front porch, the big white door opened and in the doorway was a cute little girl. She was wearing an old-fashioned sailor type dress probably one that was worn by a little girl around the 1930's or 1940's. She had beautiful long curly hair. As I got closer to the porch, I was looking at the little girl, who had a big beautiful smile, and I noticed that she only had one leg. The right leg was a peg leg, while the left leg was normal. My heart sunk at this point, but I perked up as I entered the house because she certainly wasn't in any discomfort. She walked down the hall to the back of the home with me following behind her. This is when I woke up.

A few days later, we made our trip up to Montgomery County, and when we pulled up to Bob and Mary's house, I had a funny feeling that I had been here before. For some reason, I had totally forgotten about the dream I had a few days before. The house was a big white farmhouse with two white pillars in the front. The front door opened up, and out walked Mary to greet us. While in the hallway just inside the front door, Mary had asked if we wanted a tour. Of course, I said, "Yes." While walking upstairs, it occurred to me that this was the house in my dream. I then proceeded to tell Mary about my dream. She stopped suddenly, and looked right at me and said, "That's amazing." It seems that after they bought the house, they came across a few things while going through the house. They found a little girls old-fashioned boot type shoe that ties up the front. The shoe was a left foot shoe. Mary had informed me that when they found this shoe, they searched around for the other one but now she knows there probably wasn't another shoe. They also found a post card that had Adolf Hitler's picture on it and it was from Germany. The writing was in German so neither Mary nor Bob were able to read what it said. This puts this whole home in the timeframe of 1930's or 40's.

It was almost as if I got a full history lesson of the home, long before I had even seen it. When we got upstairs, Mary showed us a little bedroom that she thought was at one time the bedroom of a little girl because there were a few old antique dolls left in the closet. Mary had redecorated the room, bought more antique toys, and set them up in the room. Mary would put the dolls in the cradle as well as sitting on the bed. Each weekend that she would arrive at the house, all the dolls and toys were scattered all over the bedroom. She is certain no one had gained entrance to the house, since all the doors and windows were still in their original locked position. She genuinely feels that there is a spirit of a little girl living there.

Submitted By Arra Mowry,
Wappingers Falls, New York
Author, Case Manager and Paranormal Investigator for
Poughkeepsie Paranormal

# CHAPTER ❧39❧

## SHADOWS AMONGST US

On January 19th, 2013, investigative teams IndyPara and Poughkeepsie Paranormal were investigating a local Bed and Breakfast called *Garrison House*, located in Fort Montgomery, NY. Owned and operated by Holly Gokey.

It was well into the night and getting close to January 20th. The team members were all on a break which is required frequently to break when on extended investigations to keep our minds sharp. I was walking in the main living room when the owner, Holly, came in the front door with the caretaker, Nicole, and with one of the Co-Founders of Indy Para, Donna, walking behind her.

Holly and Nicole walked into the dining room, but Donna turned to her right and walked into the Rose Room. Since I was teamed up with Donna most of the night I turned to follow her into the room but when I did, she wasn't there. I was quite confused so I came back out assuming I missed her. I asked the Holly where Donna was and she replied she didn't know. I again asked her, "When you came in the front door with Nicole and Donna, did you see which way Donna went?"

Holly's response was short and simple, "Only Nicole and I came in the front door. Donna was not with us."

Well, that certainly was weird. These two ladies walked in, and an apparition walked in with them that resembled Donna. Same height, dark clothing, shoulder length dark hair. The direction the apparition went should have led it directly in front of one of the IR (Infra-Red) video camera that was set up by Poughkeepsie Paranormal. I asked Jimmy, the founder of Poughkeepsie Paranormal to review that camera footage, frame by frame, to see if he can see that apparition passing in front of the camera. The apparition apparently disappeared before getting directly in front of the camera. This just goes down as being a personal experience without evidence.

Submitted By Arra Mowry,
Wappingers Falls New York
Author, Case Manager and Paranormal Investigator for
Poughkeepsie Paranormal

For more information on The Garrison House here is their website link: http://www.thegarrisonhouse.com/

# CHAPTER ❧40❧

## COMMUNICATIONS FROM A HIGHER LEVEL

Sometimes those with disabilities have a higher sense of communication, with a higher Vibration, as you will read in this story, written by Maria Murphy. It is about her personal chilling experience, and the way it changed her life forever. She now is one with the Paranormal, and has since become a paranormal investigator. She continues to search for the answers that keep her awake at night.

We moved into our home around 2003. There was a lot happening as we did a lot of remodeling (we now know that ghost's don't like change so to speak). Sometimes, I would hear a baby cry, when there was no infant in our home, I'd see a young girl with curly blond hair always passing behind me and disappearing, or I'd hear young children run up and down the hallway. Even our cat would always seem to be looking down the hallway as if fixed on something or someone.

My oldest daughter has cerebral palsy but mentally is totally fine. She uses forearm crutches to walk. She was always saying that she saw things in her room at night. One morning she woke up and said that she dreamed that Aliens were coming and they were trying to take her brother. She was truly frightened by this. I went through the whole story that aliens aren't real (or are they?)

The following morning she really was not herself at all, and the next day was almost in her own little world, and told me that it looked like the world was dying. She was 16 years old at the time. I ultimately ended up taking her to the hospital, where she almost looked and acted 'comatose.' I don't know how else to explain it.

She would wake up screaming, wouldn't eat, and started to wet herself. Ultimately, the hospital didn't know what else to do for her, so they sent her to a rehabilitation center for people with anger management problems. I fought to get her out of there, where they were treating her like a troubled teenager, and just bring her home, with me. I won that battle after two weeks.

I brought her home, but she did nothing but drool, which she never does! Then she would stare into space and start screaming until I returned. I had to get her up, feed her, shower her, change her, occupy her, and then even tuck her into bed and sleep with her. She would always lift the blanket, look down her length of her body, and then lower the blanket again.

NONE of this was 'normal' for her at all ever in the 16 years of her life. Finally, one night when tucking her into bed, and feeling total exhaustion both mentally and physically myself, I laid my head in her lap and cried aloud and I begged and pleaded with God to please give me back my little girl. I tucked her in and we went to sleep.

The next morning I woke up and looked at her and her eyes opened and she said, "Good morning Mom." All of a sudden, for some reason, she wasn't drooling anymore, and was able to do everything herself again. She even started to listen to music, read her books, and sleep in her own bed again. I felt so relieved.

A few nights later, I went to bed and fell fast asleep. My husband and my son were in the living room watching a movie. All of a sudden, there was a VERY HARD jolt of my shoulder, and I awoke to find a very dark figure, with the blackest eyes I have ever seen, and pointy teeth, and scraggly hair right in my face. I pulled the pillow from under my head and started to scream, but I couldn't chase it away with the pillow. It seemed to be there, until my husband was able to get to our room and turn the light on. It had then disappeared. This shook me so hard that I would not go into that room for three months. My son told me that the weirdest part was that the minute that I started to scream the television in the living room went out as well.

Through the previous owner of the house, I did a little research and found out that they also experienced an incident in the same bedroom. They told me their son woke up screaming one night that aliens were trying to take him. After that, their son was doing automatic writing at times. He would also say that children were chasing him down the hallway. Their son has since died in a fire. Unfortunately, they tell me that all of the automatic writing he did seemed to evolve around an old farmhouse that used to be here, and had burned. They said the automatic writing that he did went into flames with him when he died in the fire.

Submitted by
Maria Murphy,
Indian Lake, New York
This Is My Ghost Story and Why I am A Paranormal Investigator.

# CHAPTER ᴔ41ᴤ

## SERENDIPITOUS SPIRITS

**Serendipitous Spirit Number 1:**

I was probably about 15 or so when I was at a sleepover at my friend's house, an old Victorian in a valley in Stony Point (they no longer live there.). My friend, her sister, and I were all chatting, as girls do. I was in the trundle; I guess you would call it that, the part that rolls out of a trundle bed. I didn't raise it up on its legs, but, I was perfectly comfortable sleeping near the floor.

Just as we turned off the light for the night, we felt a strong draft come into the room from the hallway, between my bed and my friend's, towards the bay window, which was closed. We felt like something brushed against the bedcovers as the draft went past. At the same time I felt someone grab my upper arm. I said to my friend's sister, "Turn on the light. TURN ON THE LIGHT!"

She turned on the light and we saw nothing, but there were finger marks on my upper arm. We figured it was their younger brother, playing a trick on us and we were NOT amused. We all went out into the hallway, to hunt down the culprit. He was nowhere to be found. My friend's mom heard all the commotion, and came out to investigate. She said, "What's wrong?" We said, "WHERE'S BILLY?" (Not his real name). She said, "Why, what's going on?" My friend said, "Never mind that, just WHERE'S BILLY?" Her mom said, "He's not here, he's up at his friend Eddie's house tonight."

By this time I was inexplicably shivering, to the point where I couldn't speak properly. The finger marks were still there. We never did find out what really happened, but I bowled really well the next day with that arm!

**Serendipitous Spirit Number 2:**

We bought our house, an older home, about 20 years ago. Not too long after we moved in, Tom & I both saw most of a man standing next to the steam pipe in the living room. In broad daylight! I say most of a man because we saw he was wearing jeans and a work-type shirt, but we did not see a face. For some reason it didn't unsettle either one of us.

## Serendipitous Spirit Number 3:

Sometime after that, I was sitting in the dining room early in the morning, eating a bowl of cereal. Tom was upstairs in the shower. Our dog at the time, a Chow Chow, started barking very urgently, looking up at the stairway landing. I got up to see what was going on, figuring one of the cats was teasing her again, but I didn't see anything so I just told her to relax, there was nothing there, and she settled down. Five minutes later, Tom came downstairs and asked, "Did you just knock on the bathroom door?" I said, "Are you sure it wasn't one of the cats just rubbing against the door or something?"

He said that he heard a definite rapping on the door as if I needed to get his attention. I put two and two together and started laughing, ""I don't know who was knocking on the door, but whomever it was, Angelique was barking her brains out at them!"

## Serendipitous Spirit Number 4:

The most obvious experience I had must have been around ten years ago. It was late summer, still warm enough to sleep with the windows open at night. At 2AM, I was awakened very suddenly, by a very loud voice. All it said was a long drawn out "HI," then all was quiet. Tom was asleep. Our dog was asleep. Our cats were asleep. Apparently, I was the only one that heard it.

I turned over and looked out the window, in case it was a drunken neighbor or some other logical explanation. Didn't see or hear a thing. The scary part was that the voice had sounded like it was coming from *between Tom's pillow and mine*. I didn't tell anyone for a couple of weeks, because I truly thought I was losing my mind. Finally I got the courage to tell a close friend of mine what happened.

As I was relating the story to her, her eyes were getting bigger and bigger, and I was thinking, "Oh, great, she thinks I'm ready for the Looney bin." The real reason she had that look on her face, as she told me, was that she had heard the *same* voice say the *same* thing, and her husband and pets did not hear it either. She lived in a completely different town, and her home was not an older home.

We never figured out who that could have been that visited both of us and said the same exact thing.

Submitted by: Gail Newcomb, Rockland County

Donna Parish-Bischoff

# CHAPTER ❧42❧

### PENNIES FROM HEAVEN

I was always a spiritual soul. Maybe it was because my mother, my best friend, instilled her fascination in me. Perhaps it was because all the would be, significant women in my life (both grandmothers, my mother's sister) crossed over before I came into this world.

Whatever the reason, I was always looking for a sign that there was another place where there were souls who loved us, watching over us, comforting us. I was blessed to have my mother for as long as I did. She saw me into adulthood. She loved my two beautiful children and was there for me in good times and bad. She saw to it that I became the woman I am today.

When my mother started to get sick, she told me that when she dies, I will always know she is with me because she will leave money, coins for me to find. I said, "Oh Ma. That's just silly. I see change all over the place. You have to be more creative than that!" She assured me that I would know when it was her. Mom got sicker and I watched as she suffered. I felt tremendous guilt as I was going through a painful divorce, my son went to live with his father, and I was working and caring for my young daughter. My mother spoke less and less and eventually went into a vegetative state, never to return. I will spare the details, since I am celebrating her wonderful continued presence in my life.

Years passed. There were so many times that I cried and wished my mother were on the other end of the phone, or across the table with a cup of coffee with a sympathetic ear, and sage advice. I would find cards that she had written in my worst moments. Things like 'it gets better - I promise' would get me through the toughest times. I would see coins and "pretend" they were from my Mom. I would even tell the kids, "Look! Grandma says hello. Say hi to Grandma!" Yet, I still didn't believe it. It was still a little game I played with myself.

One day, I saw a coin in the parking lot of where I go to therapy. I said in my head, "Mom, if this is you, the date on this penny will have some significance." I admit I had some preconceived dates in my mind. Some that would "prove" that this was real. I never expected what I was to find. The date on the penny was 1968 - the year I was born.

The year my mother and I first laid eyes on each other. You can't get more significant than that! The same year, on my daughter's birthday, I saw a penny on the ground. I picked it up, threw it down, and quickly retrieved it. The date on the penny was 1999 – the year of my daughter's birth. I gave it to her that day and said, "Grandma says, Happy Birthday."

Grandma is with us and always will be.

Submitted by: Kristin Petrilak, Mount Vernon, New York

# CHAPTER ✑43✐

## MY FAVORITE ANGEL

As a child of five years old, I, for some reason was afraid of everything. I was never exposed to anything that could cause such fears, but I was afraid to actually walk from one room to another in our house. I was afraid of the dark, afraid to be in a room by myself, etc. Funny thing though, when I was in bed at night, I saw angels floating up by the ceiling, and bubbles. The bubbles were transparent.

I would call my mother into my room to show her my visitors. My mother always said they were there to watch over me and keep me safe. I accepted her explanation. I can remember just lying in bed watching my guardians float effortlessly around my room and they made me feel at peace. This was not an every night occurrence and that was okay because I always knew they would return.

At one point they didn't return for a while. It was just beginning to get warmer, and summer was ready to take over spring. This one particular evening I remember asking the angels where they were, and why they haven't come back. The following night my angels were back but they had a very well dressed man with them. He had on a dark blue pin striped suit, with a white dress shirt, and dark shoes. He was lying on his side, his hand holding his head, and he looked quite comfortable. He had a very pleasant face. For some reason, this new person didn't scare me, but I did mention him to my mother. I was again comforted by her words.

This small group of angels visited often, floating by the ceiling in front of my bed. The nice looking, well-dressed man was in different positions quite often but the one I remember the most was him lying on his side. As I got older, my visits from them slowly, went away.

Years passed, and when I was around eleven years old, I recall going through old photographs with my mother, who was trying desperately to arrange them into some sort of order. Her parents, my grandmother and grandfather, who lived on the first floor of our two family house, were also upstairs with us having coffee. My father's mother and father lived in Brooklyn, although I only knew my grandmother, since my grandfather had passed seven years before I was born. So I never saw him. As we were having a great time looking at all these old photos, one in particular caught my eye. It was of both of my grandmothers together. I noticed how they were always dressed up and how pretty their clothing was. Under that picture was another one, it was of both of my grandfathers. My heart nearly pounded out of my chest! My well-dressed angel was in the picture with my maternal grandfather! "Oh my gosh!" I thought to myself. My paternal grandfather was my angel!

He was the well-dressed man who visited with the angels! I couldn't wait to dig through more pictures to see my Grandpa. At that time the visits had stopped, and I didn't think much about it anymore until that day. Thinking about this story has always put a smile on my face. I still have the picture that, at such an early age, made me a believer in the afterlife.

Submitted by Elisa Reale, Hyde Park, New York

Donna Parish-Bischoff

# CHAPTER ❧44❧

### DAD COMES FOR A VISIT

Shortly after my dad passed away, as I slept, I remember having a dream, where I was being watched. I jumped from my sleep, and spun my head around, to see who was watching me, when I noticed a "VERY" bright light coming from the door, which, happened to be closed.

As I looked towards the door, seeing this light, I remember saying "What the fuck?", and at that very moment, the light had vanished.

You may ask, "What makes this strange?" My room, which is in the basement of my house, has two windows, neither of which lets in any light. One window, has an air conditioner permanently bolted in the frame, the other is heavily tinted. So, was this my father? Was he stopping by to check on me and my family again?

Submitted By Danny Scavone, Yonkers, New York

# CHAPTER ❧45❧

## FATHER KNOWS BEST

The house I live in and own is a two family home. My sister and her husband rent out the second floor apartment. On Friday nights, a few of our friend's, my sister, her husband, and I hang out in my sister's apartment. We drink, watch movies, smoke some cigars, and so on.

One night, as the kids slept on the third floor of the house, we all heard the stairs to their room creek as if someone was headed down to the living room. We all looked towards the hallway waiting for a child to appear, but no one showed up.

My sister got up and headed towards the hallway. She saw no one, so she headed up to the kids rooms to check, and make sure that the kids were sleeping and sure enough, all three were in bed. When she got back to the living room, she said to me, "Dad must have been checking on the kids," and we both laughed knowing that our house has spirits.

One of our friends, Billy, looked at us saying, "What do you mean by that?" We explained to Billy that in the past, we have heard and seen ghosts. We each told him some of our personal experiences in the house, and after we finished, he told us, "You're full of shit. There are no such things as ghosts."

With that, Billy noticed it was one thirty am and said he needed to head home. Less than two minutes after Billy left, my sisters' Nextel phone chirped. It was Billy. He wanted to know what we wanted. The four remaining adults in the living room all looked at my sister's phone puzzled. She chirped him back asking, "What you are talking about Billy?" we were all still in the living room. He said, "One of you guys is banging on the dining room window." My sister explained again, "We are all in the living room. Not one of us has left the room." He then chirps us back saying, "Never mind, got to go."

A few days later, when Billy went to my brother in law's auto shop, my brother in law asked him what the hell he was talking about Friday night with that phone call. Billy explained to Gregg, as he headed to his car, he heard banging on the dining room window. That's why he called us and then looked up at the window, that's when he said he saw my dad in the window and dad waved at him. He said it freaked him out and he just needed to get away from the house.

Although I've never asked him, I'd think Billy is now a believer in ghosts.

Submitted By Danny Scavone, Yonkers, New York

# CHAPTER ∾46∾

MOVING DAY

In 1977, when we moved to Yonkers, one day while I was in school, my mom was home alone unpacking from our move. After she put the dining room together, she moved into the kitchen. She returned to the dining room to get some more items that belonged in the kitchen and realized that all the dining room table chairs had been pulled from the table.

She pushed all the chairs back under the table and returned to the kitchen. She again went back to the dining room and once again, found all the chairs, pulled away from the table. She said that she now knew something was wrong with this house. She told me that she announced loudly, "I don't know who you are, but please stop messing with my chairs, and you can stay here as long as you don't harm me or my family."

The chairs never got pulled from the table again.

Submitted By: Danny Scavone, Yonkers, New York

Donna Parish-Bischoff

# CHAPTER ❦47❧

## A MOTHERS UNDYING LOVE

My mom passed away suddenly, leaving everyone in my family in shock. I think she wanted her children to know that she would always be with us, and that she was ok, and safe.

The first sign from my mother, after her passing, were birds. When the Rabbi finished with his prayers at her burial site, the birds were with us. On the ride after the services, the birds were over the high way as well, as though they were following us.

I remember one bird in particular, so different looking from the rest. I never witnessed a bird of this variety in the East Coast. I knew somehow it was my mother sending us all a message. She was telling us, flap your wings and fly! Continue your life, and I am always with you.

When she passed, as her children, all of our lives changed. In fact, I still believe the world had changed... for the better because she looked out for everyone and everything. She loved life, especially her children. To let us know she was ok and watching, she would open shades, light flickered, phones rang, things magically moved, or just disappeared, and magically reappeared.

The most powerful thing to let us know she was still around us and still to this day over twenty years even in areas with no flower's you would smell these beautiful flowers all around you but only for a few passing seconds, then it would be gone, and you would know she is watching. We, her children, would listen for her hidden messages of wisdom and love.

Wow, I just finished writing this, went to go get my cell phone, waiting for my husbands' phone call, and I went into the other room. All of a sudden, and from over my head, from a very tall stack of DVDs my husband has, a bottle of mosquito spray sprung off the shelf flying off in front of me! Mommy just wanted me to know, she felt my words, and still and always will be here, with me. I said, thanks Mom, I love you too.

Submitted by: Anita Schwartz –Michaux, Carmel, New York

# CHAPTER ∽48∾

## A VISIT FROM RAINBOW BRIDGE

A few weeks ago I was cleaning my townhouse and I moved Bones' ashes from the corner of the fireplace mantle to the center. Bones is a cat I had some time ago. Touching it made me start thinking of my little buddy. He was my best little buddy and with me for almost 13 years. He died about four years ago. It is still hard for me to think about at times. I still miss him madly. Pets are special friends. They have a special bond with us that just cannot be explained.

Anyway, I smiled and shed a few tears, as well as told him, "I still miss your 'ghetto fab' attitude." Later on in the day I went to feed BB. BB is the new cat I adopted since moving here to Kansas City. In the kitchen there was a photograph of Bones that I normally have on the window ledge. When I lived in New York in my old apartment, this photograph used to be on the floor, near Bones' food dish. Yes, I kept a picture of him near his food dish. After Bones passed, that picture remained there for when Bear, and for a short time, Zeus, ate. Bear and Zeus were two other cats that I had adopted. They were walking the floors, once walked on by the legend, so they NEEDED to know who Bones was.

Here, in Kansas City, I never put that picture near BB's food. Well, on this day I did and when BB saw the photo, he got all freaked and wild on me. It was very unlike him to behave this way. He was hunched, fat tail, puffy hair, ears back.... staring at the photo in confusion. I was like, "Dude, it's a freaking picture why all the drama?" He would NOT go near the food nor would he go anywhere near the picture?

I was like, "Whatever," so I moved the picture back to window ledge and then BB was fine and ate his dinner. Later on that night, it was time for bed. Every night it is the same thing, I call out, "It's bedtime," and little BB runs up the stairs with me and jumps on the bed while I get ready for bed. His behavior is almost dog-like. Well, on this night he runs up the stairs with me like normal but stops dead at the doorway. He will NOT come into the bedroom; he is all hunched again; his tail and hair puffy again, neck stretched like a giraffe. He was behaving EXACTLY the same way he had about 8 hours earlier when he looked at the picture of Bones near his food bowl.

So I am now lying in bed and BB still refuses to come into the room. He is freaking out, outside in the hallway, moving slowly, obviously upset by something and poking his head in and out the room without coming in. So I attempt to a take a few pictures of his bobbing head for fun, and low and behold, I look at the first picture and there is an orb in the doorway near the floor. I was like, "What the fuck is that?"

I had read and heard about what orbs are, what they could mean, but it is hard to believe in spirits and things like that. So I snap another photo within seconds of the first and the orb is there again, this time moving out of the room from where it was in the first picture I say to myself again, "WTF." I cannot see it with my eyes, only when the picture is taken is it visible?

I take a third photograph seconds after the second and the orb is gone. Then a fourth picture seconds after the third... had gone. Immediately BB recomposes himself and comes into the room as if nothing is wrong now. He looks around, up, down, left, right, and then jumps on the bed as he usually does and falls into his usual curled up position and falls right to sleep.

My friends say my bestie, Bones, came to visit. That he popped in to say hello to BB and let me know he is fine. I want to say "No way, I'm an adult, I'm rational, and this can't be. It can't." Truth is, I have never taken photos where I had orbs appear before. I have not seen any orbs since that time in any of my pictures. Maybe there is no answer, maybe there is...But it is what it is. And whatever it is, it made me remember my best little buddy—my "ghetto fab Brooklyn born legend named Bones"—the most famous cat in financial publishing.

Story Submitted By: Robert Tonchuk, Kansas City, MS

Robert took this photograph that evening

Donna Parish-Bischoff

# CHAPTER ✎49✎

## OUT OF BODY EXPERIENCE

When I was a child, for a short time, we moved into my grandparent's house. My mother and father both had alcohol problems and would fight a lot. I did not have the best situation growing up under these conditions. I can remember the violent fighting. I am not sure for what reason, but we had all moved into my grandparent's house.

I remember my room upstairs it was right across from where my mother and father slept. One evening late at night, I awoke out of my sleep. I felt as if my back had gently bounced off a wall, not hard, but as if a balloon would rise and gently hit the ceiling and bounce a little, this is the motion that had awoken me. I awoke in terror and confusion. I lay in the same position that I was sleeping in, and found myself (or my soul) suspended in mid air, all the way up to the ceiling, floating. I was confused and wondered if this was some kind of dream, keep in mind, at the time I was around the age of four or five. So, I am trying to rationalize this situation with my four or five year old mind, thinking what could be happening to me.

I start to look around my entire room. I was prone to night mares and was permitted to sleep with the light on. As I gently bounced on the ceiling, I was confused and looked around my room trying to figure out what was going on. I looked at all the toys that I was playing with that evening they were all in the exact place that I had left them.

I peered over at my rocking horse that was against the wall and all the things and I noticed everything in great detail. The position of the truck that I was playing with, the cup of water on my nightstand. It was not like a dream, but more reality.

As the thought entered my mind, saying in my own head, "How can this be a dream, I am seeing everything in such detail, this is too real to be a dream". Then the last thing that I looked at was my bed. To my surprise I saw this little boy lying in my bed curled up with his knees tucked up to his chest, lying in his side. Both of his hands under his head sleeping contently, the boy was me! Now I am really starting to think (and I tell you, I am 42 years old now and remember this just as it occurred like it was yesterday)! I start to think, "If I am up here floating, then how can my body be down there still sleeping???" Just as I thought this, all of a sudden I had this sensation of falling, as if the gravity of earth kicked in again and I gasped with fear as I started to fall. I awoke in my bed and panicked. I remember waking up in the same position that I had just seen myself in when I was up on the ceiling. I told my mother and father of this, and they would not have it at all. I became so upset that they did not believe me and continued to tell the story begging them to believe what had happened to me, that finally my mother had brought me to four different psychiatrists, she was worried about me.

All four of them said, "Janet, I don't know what to say, your son is very upset by this and I don't believe there is anything wrong with him and don't feel that he is doing this to get your attention. He has told four different doctors the same exact story to a "T" with no difference to it at all each time he tells it and he tells it with great urgency, this is not like a five year old boy to do something like this. We were expecting him to leave out some kind of detail and were watching his body language to see if he could be making this up for attention. Your little boy is telling this story in exact perfect detail time after time and crying that we believe he is sincere and not doing this for attention."


Submitted by: Chad Wellington, Bridgeport CT

# CHAPTER ∽50∾

## WAKELEE AVENUE HAUNTING SHELTON, CONNECTICUT

My wife and I had taken this rent in an old two family house. The house itself, was way over 100 years old, maybe from the early 1900's or a bit older? We did finally get the rent and moved in.

I had noticed that the house was very big, and the inside rooms very open, that is one thing that we admired about it. It also had this feeling about it when you went in, a combination of despair, sadness, and wanting to leave a little bit. On the other hand, we did like all the space that we had, rooms being very big and open. The kitchen was huge with many cabinets, so much room that we were not use to. I liked the old man of this house, but I never did like the wife, her name was "Ronny".

Of course, as I said before, I did like to smoke pot from time to time and she must have smelt this when I attempted to light up in the house. The strange thing about it is she would detect the smoke almost immediately after I blew out the first puff of smoke. They lived upstairs and the smoke would need time to travel upstairs before her detecting it. I know it was a very old house so maybe there were cracks and seams that would allow the smoke to travel up there, but literally after the smoke would leave my mouth, I would hear her upstairs yelling, "That's it Greg, you call them and you call them right now!" I fucking hated this bitch!

We only planned on staying here a year before moving on. We had so many experiences from day one. My wife is or used to be a skeptic with all of this paranormal stuff. On the first day of living here, my wife was hanging curtains in the kitchen when suddenly she came running into the living room. I could see all the blood was washed out of her face and saw that she was shaking. She called to me and when I saw her, I was alarmed of her state.

I took her with both of my hands and held onto her by her shoulders and said "Deana, what's wrong, are you alright?" She said to me, "I was hanging the curtains and saw someone out of the corner of my eye, I thought it was the landlady upstairs and was pissed that she was bold enough to just enter our living space without even knocking. I turned to address her and noticed that it was a woman not of this time period, she was dressed in Victorian clothes and had her hands contently in front of her and smiling with approval watching me hang the curtains. Then she just faded away!" This was our first encounter.

Back then my wife and I argued much about money, I use to drink a little bit and that did not help the situation; I no longer drink at all. It seemed that what was in that house did not like me; I seemed to be the target. I was in bed one night and the only way that I can describe this is having the whole weight of the world, the whole weight of planet earth getting ready to bear down on my chest. A very strange sensation, but it felt like something of huge size getting ready to just come down on top of me and crush me. I was paralyzed with fear and found enough strength to scream out; it was a terror that I have never felt before and have not felt since. For that instance I felt the fear of 10,000,000 little kids' nightmares. It was a fear that was so pure and primal, deep from within. It is so hard to describe it but it was the worst terror in my life of the purest form.

Upon my screaming out loud, "NOOOOO!" it went away and my wife woke up next to me to calm me, and asked what happened and I explained to her. Another time I was in the living room on my own, my wife had gone to bed, and I was wide awake, I don't sleep all that well, and am not a dozer, I wish I could be. When I go to bed, I am normally awake for at least an hour before I can relax my mind and body enough to go to sleep. I was sitting, watching T.V. and saw this pin size circle of smoke appear, about the size of a dime in midair off to the left and mid height of the room.

It was the kind of smoke like ribbon candy. If you ever smoked, and did not inhale but let the smoke stay in your mouth and opened your mouth to let it float and billow out, that ribbon type form it takes, this is the kind of smoke that was materializing in front of me. It slowly branched out like roots of a tree, got to about half the size of a Frisbee and then just faded into nothingness.

Again, I was wide awake and not half asleep on the couch. During the broad daylight, I would see our cat look up in the air, his tail would bush out (a cat has to be very upset for the tail to bush up like that) and his hair would stand up. The animal would back up with ears folded back and then run down the hall into the other room as if it had seen something that truly terrified it. Sometimes, we would come home from work, and I would have to get on my belly and coax our poor cat out from under the bed. He would finally come out, but not quickly, he came out very, very slowly, as if not trusting my reassurance. He would look from right to left and all around him slowly coming out as if something was terrifying him all day long, not just spooked, but total fear. This really pissed me off; whatever it was must have been scaring our cat Jasper all day while we were at work.

Other times we would come home from shopping. We would start to put our groceries away. I would go to put toilet paper and toothpaste in the bathroom and would notice this odor. I would ask my wife, "Do you think that old bitch upstairs is that rotten that she would put her cats litter box right next to the vent upstairs so that the stench of it comes down into our living space???" I would go back to the kitchen where the groceries were to get another bathroom item to put away; we are talking a matter of five seconds. The smell would be entirely gone, as if it was never there to begin with.

The smell is only one I can describe as a cat's litter box that had not been scooped in about one month, horrible. This was the most significant episode for me, how could such a horrible smell be there then I would go back to the kitchen for another item within 5 seconds and there would be no odor at all? It smelt like decay. I worked in a cemetery as a young teenager and had to go to the mausoleum and have to take way all the old flowers that were left by loved ones (I never liked doing it, thought it was disrespectful to remove the flowers but it was my job to take them after they wilted and died). When you first walk in, you can smell the pungent smell of decay and death for a brief second, then the deodorizers would kick in, but for that first moment you walked in, you could pick up on it only for a second—that is the smell that was lingering in the house from time to time.

One night, my wife and I were sleeping in bed and all twelve cabinet doors in the kitchen simultaneously started to violently open and close very rapidly. My wife and I both awoke to this early in the morning, maybe it was around two or three in the morning, and we both reluctantly went out to investigate. We made our way to the threshold of the kitchen and it just stopped. We walked through the kitchen looking at all the cabinets and made our way to the dining room. As soon as we crossed the threshold of the kitchen and entered the dining room, out of the kitchen, right behind our backs it started all over again. We went back to our bed in fear and tried to sleep.

I have seen black triangular shapes move slowly by in our room as if it were an ice berg floating by. The blackness of this shape was blacker than the black of the room around it.

Until this day, The Wellingtons have not found the source of this entity.

Submitted by Chad Wellington, Bridgeport, CT

AFTERTHOUGHTS

## "As Each Crow Gathers Circling
## The Charcoal Skies, a Tear for Each Loved One Falls"

A long time ago, someone once asked me why I was so maudlin obsessed with death, dying, and what becomes of us after we after we pass away. I looked at that person for a lengthy period of time with a blank expression trying to process and digest their question. What they asked made sense in the normal light of day, to a fairly normal looking individual. Ah! But looks are quite deceiving aren't they? (Wink)

So I said the first thing that popped into my head that seemed to make the most sense to me.

"Why not? Since I was a child I have been surrounded by illness, dying and death. It is the natural process of life. Oh sure it's upsetting to go through. I am not thrilled to go through it, and its heart breaking to face it. It takes a piece of me with it every time, and yet it gives something back along with the taking at the same time. You see death is not the ending, but the beginning to a new realm of existence; a new plane of understanding. We on earth are lost and grieve the emptiness of our loved ones. We flap about like birds with broken wings trying to fly. Until (for what feels like forever to us here, is only the blink of an eye to the souls) that day we learn all over again to take flight, and regain an understanding why we were left behind, for the time has passed and has left us."

So take comfort in knowing death is not the ending. I have shared some very intimate stories of loss with you that I have gone through that have taught me that life goes on beyond the veil of death of one's physical body. I do hope that after reading these stories you may feel a little better about death.

## CLOSING SENTIMENTS

I had often wondered what my life would have been like without all of this excitement of the paranormal. Lacking the ability to see, hear, feel, or communicate with the unknown. Unable to speak about the afterlife and what happens, or what I think may happen after we die. Then, I realize, that my life would be mundane and stagnant, one-dimensional. You see in knowing what I am learning every day, from what I do, and whom I meet, helps me gather more and more information about the several layers of existence. It leaves less and less fear and more and more hope. I hopefully, am helping others as well, with their journey in understanding the spiritual world of existence. I do not have all the answers, not even one quarter of them. But after all we are all students I feel. I like documenting what I know, what I have learned, and sharing it with as many people as possible. If I am able to help one person out of one million then I feel good.

Sometimes, I will be checking my emails and out of nowhere, I am surprised by a random e-mail from someone as close as Connecticut, and as far as Greece, Bulgaria, London thanking me for sharing my emotions and stories of loss and paranormal experiences. When I read those letters, I get emotional. I really do, because I realize that I am, in a small way helping someone, on some level, not feel so alone when it comes to death and loss, or a haunting experience. I do not feel like all spirits are here to scare us, but to lead us, help us, guide us, and protect us. I have been in some clients' homes where they are not afraid, but rather would like to understand the spirit in their home better so they can have a commutative relationship with the spirit.

Very much, like a misunderstood family member, if you will, for lack of a better term. So when people ask me am I frightened to do what I do, I must say no I am not. I am not doing anything dangerous. I feel I go into a location to create a cohesive relationship, and help the spirit. Not hurt the spirit. If a living human being were standing on a ledge of a building, you would not send a unit in to have people come and shout vulgarities and insults at them would you? Well, I treat the spirit world with the same kid gloves. With love and care. So I love what I do and I do not regret any of the experiences I have endured through my life. For they have all been gift's. My awareness has been heightened. I am content in what I do. I would like you to ask yourself the same soul searching questions my friend, then, make it count for something.

As always, if you have any questions or comments, please reach me at vampirella67@yahoo.com

Peace,
Donna

## ABOUT THE AUTHOR

Donna Parish-Bischoff grew up in Yonkers, New York. She currently resides in Upstate, New York. She released her first paranormal book in 2012 "The Lee Avenue Haunting". She is a solitary Wiccan as well as the co-founder of Indy Para, paranormal investigators. Her passion is animals and writing.

Ms. Parish-Bischoff will be donating a portion of the proceeds from the sales of this book to The Dutchess County SPCA in Hyde Park, New York. They have wonderful programs and have a no kill policy. They also participate in a Hospice program for people who are terminally ill. They have on numerous accounts treated my her own pets when they have been ill.

She also loves to attend Horror conventions as well as local libraries to share her stories and do book signings, she also writes freelance articles for Hudson Valley Halloween Magazine.com ran and operated by The Halloween Queen herself, Donna Davies.

Ms. Parish-Bischoff has also worked on two films produced by Cita Productions "Surviving Evidence" and "The K-2 Killaz" where she portrays Claire, a restless spirit that inhabits the Shanley Hotel.

## CONTRIBUTORS:

Beth Abrams
Jackie Axe
Edward Bates
John Boles
Donna Davies
Lorraine Ferrissey
Lisa Fredericks
Ann Golino
Craig Junjulas
Lisa La Monica
Kelly Liebermann
Arra Mowry
Maria Murphy
Gail Newcomb
Kristin Petrilak
Elisa Reale
Danny Scavone
Anita Schwartz
Robert Tonchick
Chad Wellington

www.ingramcontent.com/pod-product-compliance
Lightning Source LLC
Chambersburg PA
CBHW071220090426
42736CB00014B/2912